Stella Austin

Our Next Door Neighbour

A Story for Children

Stella Austin

Our Next Door Neighbour
A Story for Children

ISBN/EAN: 9783744749381

Printed in Europe, USA, Canada, Australia, Japan

Cover: Foto ©Thomas Meinert / pixelio.de

More available books at **www.hansebooks.com**

Our Next Door Neighbour.

PAGE 50.

OUR NEXT DOOR NEIGHBOUR.

A STORY FOR CHILDREN.

BY
STELLA AUSTIN,
AUTHOR OF "STUMPS," "SOMEBODY," "RAGS AND TATTERS,"
"PAT," ETC.

LONDON:
J. MASTERS AND CO., 78, NEW BOND STREET.
MDCCCLXXXI.

LONDON:
J. MASTERS AND CO., PRINTERS,
ALBION BUILDINGS, BARTHOLOMEW CLOSE, E.C.

Dedicated

TO THE VERY DEAR GRANNIE OF EIGHTY-THREE,

MRS. EDWARD MAINWARING,

WITH A GREAT DEAL OF LOVE,

AND AN EARNEST HOPE THAT SHE MAY LIVE FOR MANY YEARS YET

TO BE A SOURCE OF HAPPINESS TO US WHO LOVE HER,

AND TO SHOW TO ALL WHO COME NEAR HER,

HOW SWEET AND GOOD AND LOVELY

OLD AGE CAN BE.

CONTENTS.

CHAP.		PAGE
I.	Who told the Story	1
II.	The Country and a Cow	5
III.	Waiting for the Neighbour	23
IV.	From the Top of the Wall	44
V.	A Couple of Chattering Magpies	60
VI.	Looking in	72
VII.	It is all a'tween us	87
VIII.	Under Three Umbrellas	107
IX.	Grannie refuses to be Neighbourly	116
X.	From the Hole in the Hedge	134
XI.	Molly, Sibyl, and Prince Charming	144
XII.	The Room without a Door	157
XIII.	Grannie's very old Friend	178
XIV.	Getting back	193
XV.	Jacob's Little Girls	207

Our Next Door Neighbour.

CHAPTER I.

WHO TOLD THE STORY.

THIS is a story the fairies told me. Just as they told it to me do I tell it to you—word for word.

It is very nice to be a favourite of the fairies, and to have stories told you. In the first place, it is pleasant to hear the stories; and in the second place, if people find fault with them, say they are too long or too short, too improbable or very dull, then you can shrug your shoulders and say, "I have nothing to do with that, *the fairies told it to me.*"

If you want to hear the fairies' stories you must feel—well, I don't quite know how to express it, but I think the only word that means what I want to say is a pretty Scotch word—*eerie*. And the eerie feeling, so far as I can describe it, is just this.

First, you must feel a tiny bit—sad, I was going to say, but perhaps *pensive* would be better. Then you must sit down in a very large, comfortable, softly-cushioned chair, and you must not think about anything. You must try not even to think whether you *are* thinking. Then open your ears wide, and shut your eyes tight, and after awhile you will hear a distant booming sound, much the same noise the insects make when they chatter together in the lime trees in the early summer days; just a lazy, muffled, humming noise. This is the fairies bringing the story to you.

Then when they get quite close to you, you hear nothing but the story which they pour into your ears. They are such tiny people, and they have such tiny voices, that it takes hundreds of them, speaking all together, before the story can reach your ears. But they never get out of tune or time, and all their voices—though they speak so many at once,—are only like the chiming of a lovely silver bell,

        Ding, Ding,
          Ding, Ding,
        Ding, Ding,
          Dong.

And so the story goes on.

This is a useful thing to know, is it not? For if you are dull or low-spirited, or want amusing, all you have to do is to lie back in an easy chair and coax the eerie feeling to come to you. When once you feel eerie the story will soon begin.

And if you do not succeed the first time, do not give it up. Perhaps the fairies have been unusually busy, have used up all their stories, and are making fresh ones. Remember the useful little rhyme,

> "'Tis a lesson you should heed,
> Try, try, try again;
> If at first you don't succeed,
> Try, try, try again."

I feel the eeriness creeping over me and a far-off humming in my ears. Now the patter of tiny feet and the faint sweet chiming of their voices, the

> Ding, Ding,
> Ding, Ding,
> Ding, Ding,
> Dong,

like a silver bell. The story is coming, coming, coming; fast, faster, faster. Do you want to hear it? Hush! You must be very quiet, not talk even in whispers, or you will drive the fairies away.

Listen!

CHAPTER II.

THE COUNTRY AND A COW.

"CERISETTE," says a sad little voice.

"Yes, Master Arthur, here I am, dear. Do you want me?"

"It is very hot to-day, isn't it? and my head aches," says the sad voice, with a sigh at the end of it.

"What shall I do for you, my dear one?" says Cerisette, a nice-looking French maid, sitting down upon a low chair by Arthur's side, and arranging the cushions of his couch more comfortably. "There, that is better, is it not? And now I will dip this soft handkerchief in eau-de-Cologne and water, and lay it across your poor aching forehead, and fan you with this large Chinese fan. What a beautiful air it makes this warm day. Is it not doing your head good already, Master Arthur?"

"Yes, thank you, Cerisette, it does feel as if it was getting better," says Arthur, gratefully; then he shuts his eyes, and Cerisette, thinking he may be dropping off to sleep, fans him softly, and is silent.

The place is a big room in a big house in the big town of London, and the time is about four o'clock in the afternoon. The sun, who has travelled a great many miles to-day, has turned his bright face round, and is looking straight in at the windows. That is, he would be looking straight in if it were not for the red and white sun-blinds which are drawn closely down, and which he finds rather in his way. It is not every one who can bear the sun to look them in the face in summer, when he is so very hot and bright, and little Arthur with his headache and his tiredness, must have the room kept as dark as possible.

The minutes pass. There is no sound heard but the roll of a carriage now and then, and the silvery chiming of the clock upon the mantlepiece. It has just chimed half-past four when Arthur opens his eyes.

"My headache is much better, Cerisette," he says. "I need not have the handkerchief again. And please do not fan me any more, or it will make your hand ache."

"Nothing ever tires me that I can do for you, Master Arthur," answers Cerisette. "But I wish you could grow stronger and better, my poor little one. It makes my heart ache and ache to watch you as you lie, so white and tired. But there! I must not talk like this. If the good GOD pleases, I hope I shall soon see the day when you have a fine colour in your pale cheeks, and can run about and shout and dance with other children."

Arthur does not answer, except by a sad smile,

which makes the tears start into Cerisette's black eyes. She brushes them away hastily with the back of her hand before Arthur has time to notice them, and then she says cheerfully,

"But you do not know the news, my little one: the news your papa told me this morning. There is a gentleman visitor coming to see you this afternoon."

"Do you mean a doctor?" asks Arthur.

"Yes."

"So many doctors have come," says Arthur dolefully, "and they always look at me and say, 'Poor little fellow.' Then they thump me on the back and front with a trumpet, and then they give me some nasty medicine to take. But they never make me feel any better. I wish this one was not coming, Cerisette. I am so tired of being looked at. If I begged Father very much indeed not to let him come, do you think Father would mind?"

"Yes, I am sure Mr. Adair would mind a great deal," says Cerisette decidedly. "For this morning when he told me of it his face brightened all over, and he said, 'I have great faith in this gentleman, Cerisette, and I really think he will do my boy good, perhaps make him quite well and strong.' Those are your papa's very words, dear Master Arthur. I kept them in my memory that I might repeat them to you word for word as he said them."

Arthur sighs. "I wonder what he will be like," he says.

"Who can tell?" answers Cerisette cheerfully. "But if we are patient we shall soon see. The clock has just chimed the quarter to five. After it has chimed again he will be here."

"I wonder," says Arthur dreamily, "if he will be short and wear spectacles like the doctor who came last. I don't like spectacles, it is just as if four eyes were looking at you instead of two."

"No, no," says Cerisette. "Not another doctor with spectacles, oh, no. One of those is quite enough."

"But perhaps he will have a big voice and talk very loud, the same as the doctor who came upon my birthday," says Arthur plaintively. "Do you remember, Cerisette?"

"Do I not?" says Cerisette fondly. "Is there anything that happens to my poor dear lamb that I do not remember? It gave you a headache and spoilt your birthday. But this gentleman will be different, we will hope. Ah! There is a carriage stopping at the door. These gentlemen doctors are so punctual, for it is only just upon the stroke of five. Now listen, Master Arthur, and soon you will hear their footsteps coming up the stairs."

There is no need to bid Arthur to listen, for a light of pleasure steals over his face, and his lips curve into a happy smile as, with one finger pressed upon them, he turns his face round. This is the hour to which Arthur's thoughts turn from the time that his father leaves home in the morning, for this is the hour which Mr. Adair never fails, however he may be engaged, to devote to his little son. The footsteps come nearer, the door is thrown open, and Arthur, with a smothered cry of joy, twines his arms closely round his father's neck and draws down the dear face that he may cover it with kisses. Then, with a sigh of great content, he lays his curly yellow head upon his father's broad shoulder, and caresses his cheek with a small white hand.

"Arthur," says Mr. Adair, after a moment's pause, " I have brought a gentleman,—a friend of mine,—to see you."

Arthur has entirely forgotten there is any one else in the room save his father; but now that he remembers, he raises himself, and holds out his hand to be shaken. Then as he falls back among his cushions, he looks at the stranger earnestly and gravely.

He need have no fear of the spectacles, for the eyes that meet his are as brown and bright as his own ; and the voice that reaches his ear is as gentle, and quiet, and kind as a woman's—should be.

"It is curious, is it not," says the new doctor, "that you and I should have the same Christian name?"

"*Are* they the same?" says Arthur, roused to interest.

"Yes. You are Arthur Adair, and I am Arthur Courtney."

"How funny!" says Arthur; "and I was not named after Father, you know. I was called Arthur after a good King who lived a great many years ago; and Father is very fond of the poetry some one has written about him. Have you read it?"

"Yes," answers the doctor absently. Then he straightens himself, for he has been bending over Arthur, and his eyes sweep for one instant round the room.

He sees what a beautiful room it is, and how everything has been thought of that could give pleasure to Arthur. The walls are covered with lovely paintings, the windows are filled with sweet, growing flowers, the chairs and sofas are cushioned with soft cushions which invite you, by their very look, to sit down and rest upon them. In one corner stands a rocking-horse as large as a small Shetland pony, and from the bookcases story-books in gay bindings show their faces. A large table is covered by a Fort with hundreds of soldiers in different uniforms, and tiny cannons that go off almost as well as real ones,—better perhaps, because though they give a splendid bang, and smoke real smoke, they do not kill or hurt anybody. Upon the floor lies a Noah's Ark, and the animals carved out of ivory are in a heap beside it.

And the doctor's eyes from roving round the room come back to the little man upon the sofa, whose curly yellow head rests so quiet, and whose brown eyes are so pathetically asking for something that will do him good, and make him like other children. Then, for a few minutes, the doctor stands quite still—and looks at him.

But in these few minutes he is learning a great

deal about Arthur. Nobody speaks, Arthur and his father are both silent, but there is a wonderful fairy, whose name you must guess, and she whispers to the doctor the story of Arthur's life.

She tells him that Arthur has lived for seven years in that big house with no other playfellow than Cerisette, for his mother died when he was quite a baby. His father loves him dearly, but he is a grave, busy man, and he can only spare a few hours out of the whole long day, to be with his little son. Arthur has every toy he wishes for and that money can buy, but he has no one to share them with him, no brother, sister, or friends to help him make merry over his games, and he soon grew tired of inventing games with only himself to play them. It is such dreary work playing by oneself, just to amuse oneself, there is no fun to be got out of it. So, after his hour's lessons with his father in the morning are over, Arthur has fallen into the habit of doing nothing but lie upon the sofa and look forward to his father's return at five o'clock in the afternoon. When it is fine he rides, or drives, or walks,—but he only goes out because Father wishes it, and he always does what Father tells him. And he is very glad to get home again, to nestle down among his cushions and wonder if it is nearly time for Father to be back.

Not any of the gay people in the parks, not the pretty flowers that grow there, nor the shops full of things they pass on their road to and fro, ever win a smile or a look from Arthur. He is a little snail curled snugly round in his own shell, and not even putting out a horn to see if anybody is near him or not. GOD never meant people to think about themselves all day long, to live altogether for themselves as if there was no one else in the world. First, we should think of GOD, how to love Him and please Him. Next, we should think of other people, what we can do that will be kind to them and help them. Last of all, if there is any time left, we can think of ourselves. It is very hard this, hard even for grown-up people, but the more you try to follow this plan while you are children, the easier it will be for you by-and-by as the years roll on, and you find yourselves growing old.

But it is not quite Arthur's fault that he has curled himself round in his shell. He tries very hard to be a good little boy, and do everything his father tells him; and GOD, Who has been thinking a great deal about him, is going to show him the way to get out of his shell, and to be of use to other people.

And every minute the doctor has been thinking these thoughts Arthur has been watching him very closely—watching to see his hand go into his pocket, and bring out the trumpet which he knows so well, and has seen so often.

This doctor, however, does nothing of the kind. When he has been silent a while he sits down by Arthur's side, and takes his thin white hand into the grasp of his firm, strong fingers.

"Now, little man," he says cheerfully, "I hope we shall have you bonny and well in a few weeks. But I am going to give you a funny kind of medicine."

"Will it be very nasty?" asks Arthur dolefully; "I have had so much nasty medicine."

"That just depends upon yourself whether you call it nasty or not. *I* should like it."

"What is it?" asks Arthur.

"That you must find out for yourself. It is a riddle. I am going to order you into the country. Not to any part of the country, for that would do you no good, but to a particular part of the country where I know of a nice house to be let. There is a pretty garden and an orchard with an Alderney cow grazing in it. The cow can be had with the house, and I want you to run about in the garden and drink plenty of new milk and cream. There are two C's for you. Country and cow. You will remember those?"

"Oh, yes," says Arthur. "But is that the medicine? You said it was a riddle, and that is so easy—Country and Cow!"

"You will not find the medicine until you get there," says the doctor. "It is a particular kind of medicine, and can only be got where I am sending you."

"Does it grow in the garden?" inquires Arthur, with great interest.

"It does not grow in any garden, though it is not very far off," says the doctor. "But that is all I shall tell you now, the rest you will find out when you are there."

"And you really think it will do him good?" asks Mr. Adair.

"I am as sure of it as we can be of anything in this world," says the doctor decidedly. "I will talk it over with you by-and-by. The place of which I am thinking is not far from Town—an hour by rail, not more. That will suit you, will it not?"

"Perfectly," answers Mr. Adair, "for I shall be able to run down from Saturday to Monday. Arthur must go down alone with Cerisette at first, for it will be some few weeks before I can join him altogether."

But Arthur's eyes fill with a sudden rush of tears as he finds he is to be separated from his father, and he holds out his arms in a perfect wail of grief.

"Oh, Father, Father," he sobs, "do not send me away from you,—*please* do not. I would rather stay here and be ill, than go away and be well if *you* are not with me."

"Hush, Arthur!" says Mr. Adair soothingly, yet gravely. "It vexes me very much indeed, more than I can say, to see you so pale, and thin, and tired—unlike other children in fact. If it does you good, and if I wish it very much, it will be right for you to go away from me for a little while."

"Do you wish it *very* much, Father?" asks Arthur earnestly.

"Very much indeed, my boy," is the answer.

"Then I will go," says Arthur, choking back his tears and smiling—a wintry little smile.

"That is my brave boy," says Mr. Adair, patting the head covered with yellow curls. "I shall be able to run down every Saturday until the Monday. And when *my* holidays come we shall have a nice time of it together."

"But it will be very dull until then, Father," says Arthur, a wee bit dolefully.

"Wait until you get there," says the doctor. "After you have tried my medicine you may not find it so dull as you seem to expect."

"I wonder what your medicine is," says Arthur, smiling in spite of himself.

"Ah! it is indeed a puzzle. I do not think you will guess. I shall tell your father, but I shall ask him to keep it a secret."

"I shall try and guess," says Arthur.

"Now say good-bye, and go and tell Cerisette the news," says Mr. Adair.

Arthur not only shakes hands with the doctor,

but lifts up his face to be kissed, and then goes along the corridor to another room, where Cerisette is preparing his tea.

"We are going into the country, Cerisette," he says eagerly. "And I am to drink plenty of milk. There is an Alderney cow in the orchard where we are going. I wonder if one of the cows in my Noah's ark is an Alderney, Cerisette."

"I should think it is," answers Cerisette. "And did he order you any medicine, this new gentleman doctor?"

"That is the funny part," says Arthur. "It is a real riddle, Cerisette. He will not tell me what the medicine is, but I am to wait until I get there. It does not grow in the garden, but it is *near* the garden. I am so anxious to taste it. The doctor says he should like it very much indeed. What can it be?"

"Ah! what can it be?" says Cerisette, delighted at finding the boy so much brighter. "It must be very wonderful medicine, Master Arthur."

"Very," says Arthur. "You can only get it down in that country, Cerisette. I like the new doctor very much indeed."

"I am very happy," says Cerisette. "Did not I say that perhaps you would, Master Arthur?"

"He does not wear spectacles, and he has a kind voice, and he did not thump me with a trumpet. I wish he would come again. I am hungry, and I want my tea badly. Is it nearly ready, Cerisette?"

"Quite ready," says Cerisette, beaming upon him, for it is very seldom Arthur ever feels hungry or wants to eat. He generally eats—as a duty.

But I think the snail is beginning to put one of its horns a little way out of its shell. What do you say about it?

CHAPTER III.

WAITING FOR THE NEIGHBOUR.

IN a pretty village not far from London stand three houses side by side. They are not all the same size, indeed there is so much difference in them that they have been called in fun,—" The big bear, the middle-sized bear, and the little bear."

The big bear is a large red house, built very square, and with a paved courtyard around it. Not much of it can be seen from the roadside, for it is shut in by trees, but peeping over the hedge is a black board with white letters, which tells every one who passes to and fro that "this house is to be let."

The middle-sized bear is oddly built. At one time it must have been a small house with just a door, a window on each side of it, and three windows above. Then people lived in it who did not find it large enough, so they added another story. Then others who came after them added an arm shooting out in one direction, and then a leg, and so on. This makes it much more comfortable inside no doubt, but it gives it, to look at, an untidy appearance. The garden is an old-fashioned one, with gravel walks and straight flower borders. At the back of the house is an orchard, and upon the right side a smooth closely-shaven lawn slopes down to a tiny river, which on fine sunshiny days looks like a silver ribbon winding in and out of the fresh green grass.

And squeezed in between these two large houses is a long low cottage, with a verandah running all round it. This is the little bear. But though small, it is not to be despised, for it is prettier than either of its grander neighbours. There is a path leading up to it, and over this a trellis work has been raised, and roses of every colour and shade have been coaxed to twine themselves round about it, and form a beautiful covered archway, which in summer time is perfectly lovely. It is just as though somebody was being married every day to walk up this path and have the roses showering their blossoms upon you,—dark red satiny leaves, shining creamy ones, pale pink, bright pink, flaming crimson, rich yellow, and some as white and soft as drifting flakes of snow—you crush them under your feet as you go along.

Then the garden is so full of flowers that it is difficult to know which to pick, and which to leave. You come upon such pretty surprises too, for there are little wooden and wicker chairs so cunningly arranged under drooping branches of trees, that you do not see them until you find yourself nearly sitting down in them. Jacob, the old gardener, is very proud of this garden. He says it is "like a picter what has a good many sides to it."

Though these three houses are sometimes called for fun "The Three Bears," yet they have three real names belonging to them.

The big bear is The Red House.

The middle-sized bear is Riverside.

The little bear is Shadie Cottage.

And now to go on with the story.—

It is one of the longest days in the year, and the sun has made up his mind to have a very good time, and not to go to sleep until he is obliged. He is shining now, though it is past seven o'clock, almost as gaily as he did in the middle of the day. The birds are singing so loud, the roses smelling so sweet, it seems very hard to have to go in-doors such a lovely evening as this.

That is just what two little girls think who are sitting in one of those cosy seats at Shadie Cottage. When the clock strikes half-past seven they ought to be preparing for bed, and it is not far off half-past seven now.

The eldest of these two little sisters is seven

years old. She is short for her age, and very plump. Her face is round and rosy, a pair of large, roguish, dark blue eyes shining out of it, and fair hair waving lightly over her forehead and nearly falling into her eyes.

Sibyl, more than two years younger than Molly, is taller for her age and much slighter. Her face is thinner, and her eyes instead of being blue are a shadowy green. Her hair is several shades darker than her sister's, and curls in natural curls over her neck and shoulders.

They are both dressed alike in brown-hollands with broad crimson sashes, and their heads and necks are well covered by two large sun-bonnets, which protect them from the sun. They are out so much all day long that these are quite necessary.

For some time these two sisters have been sitting hand-in-hand, both their faces turned towards Riverside. The chimneys and the upper windows are all they can see of it from where they sit, for a grey stone wall divides their garden from their neighbour's.

"It is just one, two, three, four, five," says Molly, counting upon four fingers and a thumb of a very plump hand. "It just one—two—three—four,—*is* it four or *is* it five days, Sibyl, since the man took away the board with 'This house to be let' written upon it?"

"It is five days," answers Sibyl, "one, two, three, four, five."

"I think it is only four," says Molly. "Let us go back and count them. There was the day the man fetched away the board, that is one: then there was the day that old Mrs. Grey's dog broke his leg, that is two: then there was the day that little Tim fell into the water when he was getting watercress for tea, that is three: then there was the day that Uncle Edward's letter came to say he was coming himself, that is four: then there is to-day, and that makes five. But Sibyl, are you quite sure Jacob said that the people were coming to-day?"

"Quite sure, sister," says Sibyl.

"Why didn't you ask him what time they were coming, and who they were, and what they were like, and all about them?" says Molly.

"'Cause he said he couldn't answer any more kestons," says Sibyl, with a pout. "He was dreadfully c'oss."

"He is often cross," says Molly quietly. "Grannie says it's his complaint that makes him cross. I never can remember the name of Jacob's complaint. It is something that begins with a donkey."

"I don't 'member the name," says Sibyl. "But do you think it is his complaint what coughs so quare, sister?"

"Grannie says so," answers Molly.

"I hear wheels!" exclaims Sibyl, holding up a thin, sunburnt hand. "The next door neighbours are coming, sister, let us go and meet them."

They are off their seats in a second and hurrying down the rose path, treading the sweet leaves under their feet as they bound along, while a fresh shower are shaken upon their sun-bonnets and pitter-patter down upon them like great drops of rain.

Molly and Sibyl are breathless when they reach the gate. They fling it wide open and rush out just in time to see a farmer's gig coming along at a slow trot.

"Oh! It's Farmer Morton's night," says Molly. 'Why, I quite forgot!"

"So did I," says Sibyl. "Wouldn't he be sorry, sister, if he knew we had quite forgotten him?"

"We were thinking so much about our next door neighbours," says Molly.

"Good evening, little ladies," and Farmer Morton pulls up his horse. "And how are you this lovely evening?"

"Quite well, thank you. Are you quite well?" they chime in both together.

"Very hearty indeed, thank you, little ladies," answers Farmer Morton. Then giving a mysterious

PAGE 31.

nod, he says in a whisper, "Do you know what day it is to-day?"

"Midsummer Eve," shout the sisters with one voice.

"The day when the fairies are very busy," says the farmer.

"Is it only to-day they are busy?" interrupts Sibyl.

"They are more or less busy all the year round," answers Farmer Morton.

"Only to-night they wisit at each others' houses and give a grand party, and have a great deal of fun," says Sibyl.

"Well, they are very fond of making presents on Midsummer Eve to people they like," says the farmer. "And as I was passing by they gave me these presents to give to you," and Farmer Morton pulls out of his pocket four parcels, two of which he hands to Molly and two to Sibyl.

"It is so kind of the fairies," says Sibyl, dancing in a high state of glee, while Molly adds, "We ought to say 'thank you very much' to them. Shall you see them on your way home, Farmer Morton?"

"Well, they *might* be somewhere about," answers the farmer.

"Then please thank them *very* much," says Molly.

"And *very* much from me," says Sibyl. "Molly would write them a nice letter and I would draw them a pretty picture if we knew where they lived. How should we direct it, Farmer Morton? and which of the fairies sent these lovely presents?"

"Oh they don't like to be thanked," says Farmer Morton, flourishing his whip as if he were in a hurry. "Nothing offends the fairies so much as thanking them. It doesn't matter which of them it was what gave them, Miss Sibyl. It's all the same as if all the fairies had sent the presents. It's only a trifle."

"Oh, then they showed it you," says Sibyl. "You know what it is. How tight the fairies tie their parcels," and her little fingers tug at the string.

"Yes, they are uncommon good at tying up parcels," says Farmer Morton. "Now, good evening, little ladies. Take care of the dew when it falls, and don't get your feet wet," and he drives away quickly, for he is later than usual to-night, and he has a mother watching for him.

"The dew is not falling yet," says Molly, holding the dry sole of her shoe so that Sibyl can see. "The sun won't go to sleep for a long time. They have not even begun to get his bed ready, and it takes them a long while to make it properly."

"There is a bit of red blanket and a corner of a gold sheet," says Sibyl, waving her hand towards the west, where tiny streaks of crimson and amber show themselves.

"The fairies have sent us such nice presents," says Molly. "Mine is a packet of gingerbread and a workbox. Oh, what a dear little thimble, sister!"

D

"Mine is just the same as yours," says Sibyl, who has managed to pull off the string, " oh, what *'licious* gingerbread. I wonder how the fairies knew we liked gingerbread. I wonder—do you think Farmer Morton told them, Molly?"

"Perhaps he did," says Molly, who is too busy to think much about it.

"What nice needles," said Sibyl. "They have *gold* eyes to them. Look, sister."

"I hope that as they are fairy needles they will do my work better, and not prick my finger so much," answers Molly gravely. "Just see, this finger is all red and the skin torn," and she holds out a fat forefinger.

"Mine is nearly as bad," says Sibyl, as she compares her finger with Molly's.

"It is a good thing the fairies sent us these needles, or we should have worn our fingers to the bone in time," says Molly.

"That would be *drefful*," gasps Sibyl; "why we should be like the man Uncle Edward told us about, who took off his flesh and sat in his bones, *only* in his bones. Think of that, Molly."

" But you don't believe *that* story, do you ?" says Molly. " Why it was only one of Uncle Edward's make-believes, and not a real story. Don't cry, Sibyl. I am a great deal older than you, and I tell you it is not true. These needles are lovely, sister, the fairies sent them on purpose, because they knew the others were nasty and wouldn't work and pricked our fingers. Listen ! there is Maria calling us ! Oh, Sibyl, you run the quickest. Please run in and ask her to let us sit up a wee bit longer. It isn't Midsummer Eve *every* day."

" But suppose our next door neighbours come while I am away," says Sibyl lingering, and turning a pair of wistful eyes towards the chimneys of Riverside, from whence the smoke is curling gaily upwards.

" They won't, if you are very quick," says Molly, " and if they do I'll call very loud."

Sibyl lingers for a moment, and then runs off.

Molly goes back to their two little chairs, where Sibyl soon joins her,—red, panting, breathless, but in triumph.

"Twenty more minutes Maria says we may sit up, but no longer, Molly."

"That will do nicely," says Molly, settling herself comfortably. "They must come in twenty minutes. And I have thought of such a nice game to play, Sibyl. We will guess what our next door neighbours will be like, and we will see who will be most right."

"I guess they will be a nice old lady and gentleman, just the same as Mr. and Mrs. Bertram who had us in to tea so often, and loved us so much," cries Sibyl eagerly.

"What beautiful cakes they gave us," says Molly.

"And such 'licious strawberries and cream," says Sibyl.

"Those were such happy days," says Molly, shaking her head mournfully, "and such a long time ago. Two whole weeks, Sibyl! And the man was so unkind he would lock the gates, and we couldn't even get in to stroke the dear cow and tell her we were so sorry that her master and mistress were gone."

"I hope the new master and mistress will be wery kind to the dear cow," says Sibyl. "Now, Molly, I have had my guess, and it is your turn."

"I guess they will be a tall lady and gentleman with twenty little boys, some of them littler than we are, some of them bigger, and some of them the same size," says Molly boldly.

"Twenty!" says Sibyl. "Oh, Molly, what made you think of such a great many, and why didn't you make some of them *girls?*"

"Because that is what I guess," answers Molly. "But we shall soon see, for they will have to come soon."

But "they" do not. The birds, except the nightingales, hush their songs, the sun moves nearer to the lovely bed preparing for him, the dews begin to fall so thick and fast that Maria comes to hurry them in. She turns a deaf ear to all entreaties for "just five minutes more," and tells them to go at once to their grandmamma and then up stairs to her.

Grannie is the dearest old lady in a story book or out of it. She is sitting in a large arm-chair, which is quite her own, and which no one else ever thinks of sitting in. It is drawn near the window, and she has a fleecy snow-white shawl thrown over her shoulders and her snow-white hair tucked away under a snow-white cap. She has such a soft, round, kissable face, I am sure you would want to kiss her if you were to know her. She has another cap on now, a cap the sisters call "Grannie's thinking cap."

The room where Grannie is sitting is always a dark room, with odd nooks and corners, and lighted only by two small windows. To-night it is darker than usual, for the blinds are halfway down—most likely Maria has forgotten to pull them up when the sun left the room. Perhaps it is the dusky light, or perhaps Grannie with her still white face and figure looks a tiny bit like some one from another world,—perhaps it is both these things together, but certainly the sisters do not talk so boldly of the fairies now as they did an hour ago in the broad sunshine. They show Grannie the presents, and tell her the story about them in very low voices and with mysterious little nods and waving of the hands. Grannie suggests boldly that Farmer Morton had more to do with the presents than the fairies, but they are both so indignant at the mere idea that she leans back in her chair, and says,

"Well, my dears, have it all your own way. If you choose to think the fairies sent them, pray do. And if it pleases you both, *I* am quite satisfied."

"But, Grannie," argues Molly, "the needles show they are fairy needles. They have gold eyes. And they are sent to do our hemming nicely and not prick our fingers."

"If they do your hemming better, I shall not be the one to grumble, my dear!" says Grannie. "For I must say the half-side of the handkerchief you hemmed to-day was *disgraceful.*"

"That was the fault of those horrid, common needles, Grannie," speaks up Sibyl. "We tried to make them work, and they wouldn't. They broke six of themselves, Grannie, trying to do the piece of hemming you set me."

"Six! Dear me," says Grannie, "that is very wasteful. Six needles a day for you alone! Why just think what a number that would be at the end of the year!"

"It was wery stupid of them to break," says Sibyl. "I told them so, but they wouldn't 'tend to me. But these fairy needles! You will see how beautiful they will work to-morrow, Grannie."

"Indeed I hope so, my dear," says Grannie. "Now say me your Psalm, and then run off to bed. You are later than usual to-night."

With folded hands they stand before Grannie,

and say verse by verse the 23rd Psalm. Then they kiss her, and race up stairs to bed, Sibyl winning the race by a whole length of the passage.

There is a proverb which declares that "a watched pot never boils." It means that if you are watching for something, it very often does not come until you have grown tired and have given up looking for it. And so it happens to-night, for the sisters have just begun to undress, when the fly, for which they waited so long and so patiently, drives up to Riverside. If they had heard the wheels, I am sure they would have scampered down stairs, with only half their clothes upon them to have a peep at "our next door neighbours." But luckily they hear nothing. They have won a hard-fought battle and are jumping about in high glee. They wake very early in the morning, somewhere about four o'clock in the summer-time, but Grannie has given strict orders that they are not to wake Maria to dress them before half-past six. Now they have coaxed Maria to ask Grannie if they may not get up at six o'clock to-morrow for a great treat. Grannie says 'yes,' but that they are to understand it is to be only to-morrow and not any other morning.

"It is lucky people don't take houses every day in the week," says Maria, "for you are a couple of wild Indians to-night. Now Miss Sibyl, come and have your night-dress on at *once*."

"The sooner we go to bed and to sleep the sooner the morning will be here," says Molly, sobering down. "Oh, Maria, why won't you let us get up with the sun? *He* gets up beautiful and early."

"The sun has his work to do and you have yours," says Maria. "And your work is to be good and obedient children, and to do as your grandmamma tells you."

"Grandmamma is such a *long* name," says Sibyl "I like Grannie best."

"Shut your eyes tight, Sibyl, and go to sleep," says Molly, as she nestles down in one little white bed, and Sibyl does the same in another. "It will soon be morning."

Sibyl, who is sucking her thumb to send her to sleep, murmurs, as she opens her eyes a tiny bit,

"And then when morning comes, then we shall see our next door neighbours."

CHAPTER IV.

FROM THE TOP OF THE WALL.

SUCH a great deal of work the sun has got through this morning before many people were awake. He has swept the fresh sweet dew off the grass, and dried the scented hay that is lying about. He has fallen upon the grey sea and broken it up into thousands of silver ripples. He has kissed the buds into full-grown flowers, and warmed the earth, and ripened the fruit. Oh, there is no end to the beautiful work the sun has been doing this morning, and now he is staring very hard at Molly and Sibyl as they stand talking together.

They are too busy to think about him at all, only as he comes in their eyes, in spite of their large sun-bonnets, they go blinking, blinking, blinking, like a couple of dear little white fluffy owls just brought into the sunshine.

"I know where Jacob has left the short ladder," Molly is saying, "but one short ladder is not much use. You would like to see as soon as me, wouldn't you, sister?"

"Oh, yes," answers Sibyl eagerly; "of course I should. You won't go up without me, Molly? Couldn't we both go up the same ladder?"

"I am afraid we should push each other off," answers Molly. "But—oh, Sibyl, there is the hall chair what turns into steps,—you know."

"Oh, yes, let us fetch it at once," says Sibyl dancing along.

The maids are at breakfast in the kitchen, so the children have the front of the house to themselves. The chair is oak, and very heavy, and it takes them some time to push it to where they want it to go—against the stone wall which separates their garden from that of Riverside. Then they fetch the short ladder from its hiding place, and put it side by side with the chair ladder, and seat themselves down for a few minutes' rest. They are red and hot, and not nearly so clean and nice as when they left their bedroom nearly two hours ago.

"I wonder if Uncle Edward came last night," says Sibyl.

"Oh, yes," answers Molly; "he is sure to have come. He always comes when he says he will. Now, if you are rested, Sibyl, let us go up the ladder, and we shall soon see our next door neighbours,—they are sure to be in the garden now."

Step by step the two sisters mount the ladders, until they can see into the next garden. Then they cuddle their white chins upon the dusty wall, and look eagerly around them.

The smoke is curling out of the chimneys as it did last night; upon every side stretch the straight old-fashioned flower borders, while before them gleams the cool green turf with its silver edge—that narrow river running so silently along. Many a time have the sisters paddled in it, dragging out the water-cress in great handfuls, and then leaving it to bake in the sun. The old lady and gentleman who lived at Riverside for some months loved the two children dearly, and they were as much at home there as in Shadie Cottage, running all over the place like a couple of white cats. But Mr. and Mrs. Bertram have gone to live near a married son, and Molly and Sibyl are looking out for new next door neighbours.

Everything is very still and quiet this summer morning. There is no sound of any kind to be heard. No chattering voices, no pitter-patter of feet, no people big or little taking a walk in the garden.

The pair of blue eyes and the pair of green eyes search every nook and corner eagerly, quickly, brightly. Then Sibyl's face lengthens, Molly's grows very blank, and they squeeze their chins closer against the top of the dirty wall.

"Perhaps we are too early," says Molly in a disappointed voice.

"They must be wery lazy," says Sibyl with contempt; "we have been up a great while."

"Let us sit down and wait," suggests Molly.

It is difficult for two small people with very short legs to turn about on the top of a ladder and sit down upon a wall. They are quite careful, but once Sibyl nearly turns a somersault into our next door neighbour's garden. Luckily for her Molly seizes hold of her dress just in time to save her.

"The sun is shining wery hot this morning," says Sibyl fretfully; "I wish he would turn his face another way. He's looking round the corner of my sun-bonnet, and burning my cheeks *drefful.*"

At this instant the front door they are both so anxiously watching, opens, then shuts again, and Arthur, fresh from the hands of Cerisette, steps out upon the gravel path.

He awoke early this morning: so early that he heard the lowing of the "dear cow" as they milked her for his breakfast. He was so anxious to look for his new medicine, that he gave Cerisette no peace until she dressed him to let him go out.

He is dressed in a sailor suit of some soft white stuff, and a broad-brimmed sailor hat is set far back upon his yellow head. He walks slowly along, his eyes glancing right and left, as if in search of something.

Molly and Sibyl hold their breath, then Sibyl whispers gently,

"Our next door neighbour, Molly!"

"And such a *nice* next door neighbour," Molly whispers in an admiring voice.

"Grannie says we is to love our neighbours," says Sibyl, still in a whisper. "And I think Grannie would like us to love our next door neighbour a wery great deal."

Arthur is just passing under the wall.

"We will speak to him," says Molly. "Good morning, next door neighbour. Are you very well?"

Arthur jumps at the sound of the voice. Then looks about to see from whence it comes—looks everywhere but up at the garden wall.

"Here we are," cries Sibyl, "up here: upon the top of the garden wall. We have been watching for you such a long time."

"Were you not very late in getting up?" says Molly, with gentle reproach. "We have been up *hours,* and we were so anxious to see you."

"I was up *much* earlier than usual this morning," says Arthur, looking in perplexity at his strange visitors, seated at their ease upon the top of the wall. The two sun-bonnets are bent eagerly towards him, the pair of roguish, dark blue eyes, and the pair of serious green ones are taking him in from head to foot. Arthur blushes rosy-red from his slender white throat to the roots of his yellow curls.

"Are you all by yourself?" asks Sibyl.

"Cerisette came with me yesterday," says Arthur, "and the servants came the day before."

"Who is Cerisette?" inquires Molly. "Is she your mamma?"

"Oh, no," replies Arthur. "She is a French nurse. But she has been with me ever since I was born, and she speaks English almost as well as French."

"Then we shan't have to talk French to her, shall we?" says Sibyl, in a tone of relief. "'Cause we don't know it. Grannie is going to get some one to teach us wery soon."

"Shall you stay here a long time?" says Molly.

"We do not know yet," says Arthur. "If it does me good, perhaps we shall. The doctor ordered me to come into the country and drink plenty of milk from the cow."

He is about to tell them of the curious, mysterious medicine, hoping they may help him to find it, when Sibyl interrupts eagerly,

"Ah, the dear cow. We know her wery well."

"Did she belong to you once?" asks Arthur.

"No," answers Molly. "But we often went in to tea at your house when Mr. and Mrs. Bertram lived there a great while ago—before you came. And we had strawberries and cream."

"It was 'licious," says Sibyl. "The dear cow's cream is wery nice, and so is the strawberries too."

"Won't you come into our cottage and see our grannie?" asks Molly. "She would like to see you, for we have been telling her ever so many days that our next door neighbour would be coming soon."

"She isn't our grannie, but our great-grannie," Sibyl explains, "and that is two grannies in one. So that it is much nicer than *one* grannie. But great-grannie is so long to say, and we call her grannie for short."

"It is a pity you can't get over the wall," says Molly, "but there is no ladder your side. If you run down to the big gates, we will meet you and show you the way."

"I had better tell Cerisette where I am going, if you can wait," says Arthur.

"We can't wait," says Molly, "and we will bring you back quite safe. Make haste and run fast."

Arthur stands uncertain for an instant, but the bonnets have disappeared below the wall, so he follows Molly's directions, runs across the lawn and out at the iron gate.

He meets the sisters in the lane, and they take him between them, each holding a clean fair hand of his in one of their grubby brown ones. Up the rose walk they go, and the full-blown roses of yesterday merrily shake their dainty, many-coloured leaves upon the three children as they pass underneath them.

"How pretty it is, and how sweet the roses smell," says Arthur.

"Yes, arn't they 'licious?" says Sibyl, sniffing. "You must come into the drawing-room first, 'cause we have something to show you. You did not know, did you, that the *fairies* are our friends?"

" *No*," says Arthur, in a very astonished voice.

" Yes," replies Sibyl, dancing gaily on before him, "and they sent us a present, two lovely presents each. Sit in that chair and we will show them to you."

The workboxes are much admired, and a corner of the packets opened that the brown, crackling gingerbread may be seen.

" But we must not eat it until Grannie says we may," and Sibyl puts it quickly out of sight, " and we had better not give you any until Grannie says you may have it, 'tickerlarly if you have been ill," and Sibyl, who is fond of using hard words, repeats with great pride, " 'tickerlarly if you have been ill."

" Uncle Edward has come," says Molly, who has slipped out of the room while Sibyl was showing the presents. "I tried his door, and it was locked, but I heard him splashing about in his bath. Such a beautiful bath he must be having, sister, for he is making such a great noise."

"Poor Uncle Edward," said Sibyl, shaking her head. "That is 'cause he can't wash himself when he is in London. Maria says water is wery scarce in London, and when he comes here I s'pose he has to wash himself wery much to get himself clean."

"Oh," says Arthur eagerly and earnestly, "but that is not true about not getting water in London. We live in London, and I have just as much water for my bath there as I had for my bath here this morning—*quite* as much."

"Do *you* live in London?" says Sibyl. "Then of course you know our Uncle Edward. How glad he will be to see you again."

"He only lives in London part of the year," explains Molly. "He is down here staying with Grannie and Sibyl and me very often. Whenever he can spare time he runs down."

"Perhaps Father knows him," says Arthur, "but I don't think I do."

"Oh, you will 'member him when you see him," says Sibyl. "Now you had better come up and let us show you to Grannie."

"He can look at this picture-book first," says Molly.

Then they prepare to take their visitor up stairs.

"You go first, Sibyl, to show the way," says Molly, "and I will come after you with Arthur."

They reach the landings where the bedrooms are. Sibyl's fingers are closing upon the handle of a door when Molly turns to Arthur.

"You won't be frightened at seeing Grannie in a night-cap, will you?" she says. "Grannie always wears a night-cap when she is in bed, you know."

"Oh," says Arthur, drawing back, and speaking in a surprised voice. "But I would rather not go in until—until—your grannie is dressed.

She would not like it, I am sure she would not like it."

"Oh, Grannie does not mind," says Sibyl, opening her eyes wide. "She lets us run in and out."

"Are you afraid of the night-cap?" says Molly reproachfully. "I didn't think you would be."

"No, I am not," says Arthur in a distressed voice. He is too shy to explain, but he is a true little gentleman, and he feels that a stranger going in to Grannie suddenly is quite different to Molly and Sibyl running in and out. He says no more, however, and Molly seizes his hand to drag him along.

Sibyl is about to fling open the door with a flourish when a handle close by is turned and a gentleman stands in the midst of them.

"Good morning, my nieces, and what is all this noise about?" he says. "Whom have you here, Molly? I hear the fairies have been at work in these parts. Perhaps this is a fairy Prince. Little Prince Charming, eh?"

"He is our next door neighbour, Uncle," says Molly, "and we are just going to take him in and show him to Grannie."

"I am sure Grannie will be very glad to see him later on when she is dressed and downstairs," says Uncle Edward. "But now it is time for breakfast. Will Prince Charming stay and have some with us?"

"Oh, I forgot Cerisette!" says Arthur quickly and timidly. "She does not know where I am, and I ought to have told her. I must not stay any longer, thank you."

"We will send in and tell her you are here," says Uncle Edward. "I am sure you want some breakfast to bring colour into those white cheeks. You should divide your roses, Molly, and give him half."

"I would if I could," says Molly, rubbing her cheek.

"There must be something done to you both before you are fit to have breakfast with me," says Uncle Edward, looking at his nieces in disgust.

"What *has* happened to you? You might be two little pigs instead of two little girls."

This is true, for their knees are grimy, their hands black, their clean frocks soiled and crumpled, their sashes under their arms and their faces smeared by being rubbed upon the dirt at the top of the stone wall. Such a contrast they are to Arthur in his fresh white suit and with his clean fair hands and face, and smooth yellow curls.

"But we have been up so long that we have had time to get dirty," says Molly cheerfully.

"Yes, and you have only just washed, so it's no wonder you are clean, Uncle Edward," says Sibyl in triumph.

"I heard you splashing about, and making such a great noise in your bath," says Molly.

"It seems that even the walls have ears in this house," murmurs Uncle Edward. "But come to breakfast *clean and respectable*, if you can. I shall take Prince Charming with me, and then you will be down all the sooner."

CHAPTER V.

A COUPLE OF CHATTERING MAGPIES.

BREAKFAST is laid in the verandah, out of reach of the sun, but where a gentle wind blows soft kisses to them across from the roses.

"That is better," says Uncle Edward, as Molly and Sibyl appear with clean faces and hands, well washed legs, and fresh dresses and sashes. "But I wonder how long you will remain so?"

"That 'pends upon what we do after breakfast," remarks Sibyl wisely.

"Yes," says her uncle; "I fancy if I meet you in an hour, you will be like two chimney-sweeps."

"Don't you love chimney-sweeps, Uncle Edward?" asks Sibyl wistfully.

"They are very useful in their way. What made you ask such an odd question, Sibyl?"

"'Cause Jacob doesn't," says Sibyl. "He says he lived next door to one once, and he was that grimy he couldn't abide him. But *you* would love a chimney-sweep if he was your neighbour, wouldn't you, Uncle? 'Cause Grannie says we ought to love our neighbours."

"One might have worse neighbours than a chimney-sweep," replies Uncle Edward.

"Do you think you should love him well enough to kiss him, even if he was *wery* sooty?" asks Sibyl earnestly.

"I really have never thought about it," says Uncle Edward, " and it is a subject which requires a great deal of thought, Sibyl. Now, tell me Prince Charming's name when he is not Prince Charming, for I have heard you call him nothing but 'our next door neighbour.'"

"My name is Arthur Adair," answers Prince Charming for himself.

"And are you alone with your French nurse?" asks Uncle Edward.

"Father will come very soon," says Arthur; "but he cannot get away yet, because Parliament is sitting."

"How many eggs is she sitting upon?" asks Molly briskly. "Because we have a hen called Draggletail, and she is sitting upon eleven eggs."

"Parliament is not a hen," says Uncle Edward, "but a great many men who meet together in two large houses called the House of Lords and the House of Commons. They make laws, and—talk about them."

"Ah," says Sibyl, "I thought it was a quare name for a hen."

"And oh, Uncle Edward," cries Molly, laying a sticky hand upon his heather-mixture coat. "We want to ask you a question."

"Ask as many as you please," he replies, gently moving the plump hand from his coat sleeve.

"I forgot. You don't like stickiness," says Molly, "and my hands *are* rather sticky. But it's no use going to wash them, because I mean to have some more jam."

"If you please," corrects her uncle.

"If you please," says Molly meekly.

"And now what wonderful question is it you want to ask me?"

"I know," cries Sibyl suddenly. "Let me 'splain about it, Molly."

"No! no!" says Molly. "I began, and I must *ex*-plain. You are too young to *ex*-plain, Sibyl. You can't say your words p'operly. You should say *ex*-plain, not *'splain.*"

They are very fond of each other these two sisters, but they do sometimes have a tiny quarrel. Molly is rather fond of laying down the law, and Sibyl, who has a will of her own, often resents this. She likes to imagine she can say long words quite correctly, and she is very touchy upon the subject. The tears start to her eyes now, but she turns to her plate, and pretends to be eating as if nothing is the matter.

Tender-hearted Molly is not often unkind, and she is sorry for what she has said as soon as the words have left her lips.

"I will tell half, Sibyl, and you shall tell half," she says, with a repentant look at her sister.

But Sibyl does not speak.

"Come and sit on my knee, and have a big strawberry," says Uncle Edward.

She is soon herself again, and then Uncle Edward says,

"Now, Molly, go on with your story, and Sibyl shall help you with it."

"Arthur lives in London and you live in London, and you do not know each other," says Molly, "and we think it so funny that you both live in the same place and don't know each other."

"There are a great many people in London," replies her uncle, "and it is impossible in a large place like that to know *everybody*."

"How quare," says Sibyl. "Why this is a big place, and we know everybody in it. Don't we, Molly?"

"I have no doubt you do, and not only every person, but every dog, and cat, and hen, and duck, and chicken," says Uncle Edward.

"Only this year's ducks and chickens," says Molly earnestly. "Last year's ducks and chickens always grow up like the ducks and chickens of the year before that, and we never can tell them apart, can we, Sibyl?"

"No," says Sibyl thoughtfully. "But it is so quare, Uncle Edward, not knowing all the people in London."

"Not at all 'quare,'" replies Uncle Edward, "for if you remember I have told you often and shall tell you again that you are the two greatest little gossips that ever lived. No one can equal you."

"But Grannie says we are to love our neighbour," says Molly, "and she says she does not mean only our next door neighbour, but all the people around," and Molly spreads out her fat hands and waves them about.

"Yes, and now we wisit at all the houses and loves them all wery much," says Sibyl. "But we mean to love our next door neighbour the best. I am so glad he is not a chimney-sweep and sooty. Let me go back to my place by his side, please, Uncle."

"And leave me," says Uncle Edward, pretending to cry. "Oh, you changeable little woman. Another time I shall be the one to desert you."

"I don't believe you," says Sibyl, shaking her curls at him, "You will always let me come and sit on your knee when I like, *I* know."

"When you are clean," adds Uncle Edward.

"But Uncle," says Molly, too earnest about the subject to let it drop, "you can't love people if you don't know them, can you? And if you don't know your neighbours in London you can't love them?"

"But I *do* know a few people in London, and I believe I love them—some of them at any rate," replies Uncle Edward. "You have no idea what a large place London is, Molly. There are hundreds of streets, with big houses and little houses filling them up. Ask Prince Charming and he will tell you."

"Oh, yes," says Arthur. "London is a very large place indeed, and it takes a long, long time, even in a carriage, to go from one end of it to another. This is only a tiny, tiny place by the side of it."

"It is quite big enough," says Sibyl, quickly. "It takes us a *long* while to wisit at all the houses."

"Yes, I suppose so," says Arthur, meekly.

"I have not asked after my old friend Jacob yet," says Uncle Edward. "When I was here last his asthma was bad—"

"That is the word I wanted to remember," says Molly. "I was sure it began with a donkey."

"Jacob is very c'oss," says Sibyl, shaking her head gravely. "Molly wouldn't speak to him all day yesterday. He knew who was coming to be our next door neighbour, and I went all by myself to ask him. Molly wouldn't come with me."

"Oh, Molly, Molly," says Uncle Edward, seriously. "That does not seem much like 'loving your neighbour,' does it?"

Molly blushes redder, and hangs her head until her gold-brown curls hide her scarlet cheeks.

"He was so *very* rude, Uncle," she says with dignity.

"He called Molly and me bad names," says Sibyl, eagerly.

"What did he call you?" asks her uncle.

"A couple of chattering magpies," answers Molly.

"And why did he call you that?" says Uncle Edward.

"The day before yesterday it rained fast," replies Molly, "and the weeds grow up after the rain. And we thought we were doing good by pulling them up, and then—"

"Then Jacob came," puts in Sibyl, "and he was d'eadfully c'oss. He said we had pulled up the seed and left the weeds. But we thought they was weeds."

"And he said," continues Molly, "that we were quite old enough to know nasty weeds from good seed, and that we were always talking so much, and that was why we wouldn't learn which were the seeds and which were the weeds."

"And then he called us 'a pair of chattering magpies,'" says Sibyl, "now wasn't he c'oss, Uncle Edward?"

"I think it was 'a couple,' not 'a pair,'" says Molly.

"I think it was 'a pair,'" says Sibyl.

"I am almost sure it was 'a couple,'" says Molly, earnestly.

"I am *quite* sure it was 'a pair,'" says Sibyl, positively.

"Poor Jacob," says Uncle Edward, pityingly.

"What between you and his asthma he has rather a bad time of it I am afraid."

"Grannie says it is his donkey complaint what makes him c'oss," says Sibyl.

"Don't you think you may have something to do with it?" begins their Uncle Edward, but Sibyl interrupts him hastily with—

"Here is the French nurse. Now are you quite sure, Arthur, we shan't have to talk French to her?"

Cerisette, in her anxiety about Arthur, has appeared to carry him off. She says he must go in doors and rest. Later on he can come in again, if the little ladies are so kind as to want him.

The "little ladies" can hardly be coaxed to give him up. They meant to have kept him all day. But Cerisette is firm. Mr. Adair is not here, and she is responsible. But she promises Arthur shall have tea with them, and that she will bring him in about four o'clock in the afternoon.

The sisters each take one of his hands and

insist upon walking with him to his own gate. To the very last they have a hope in their hearts that Cerisette will invite them in to be with him. But she does not. Perhaps it does not occur to her. So Molly and Sibyl are left behind, their two wistful faces squeezed against the bars of the gate, watching Arthur so far as they can see him.

CHAPTER VI.

LOOKING IN.

THE sisters coax Grannie for a whole holiday, because they do not feel they can settle down to anything to-day. And their tongues never cease to talk about "our next door neighbour." Dear Grannie in her arm-chair near the window has knitted on with a patient smile, while she listens to the description they give of little Prince Charming. Sibyl takes great pains to impress upon Grannie that his eyes are the same colour as those of Mr. Strong's collie dog, and Molly says his nose is kyline. This puzzles Grannie until she finds out that Molly means *aquiline*.

They have done everything they can think of to give Prince Charming pleasure. They have gathered a large bouquet for him—running off with some of Jacob's choicest blossoms when that poor old man's back is turned. They have asked cook to make some of their favourite cakes, they have picked the fruit, and chosen the prettiest spot in the garden where they will have tea. And now they are dressed in clean white frocks with blue sashes, their hair tied with blue ribbons, and they are thinking that four o'clock will *never* come.

A quarter to four, and Molly and Sibyl stand in the middle of the drawing-room hand in hand. Their eyes are fixed upon the clock, and they are worrying Grannie with—

" Now, isn't it four o'clock, Grannie? Are you *quite* sure it isn't? You said it was fifteen minutes to four, a *long*, *long* while ago."

" Twelve minutes to four," says Grannie in a resigned voice. " I cannot make it go quicker, my dears, and I believe my watch is true time. At least so your uncle says."

"But you are not *quite* sure," says Sibyl.

"As sure as I need to be," says Grannie. "It is only a minute or two wrong, if any. Now, my dears, be patient for a short time."

For three minutes they are like mice, then Sibyl says,

"Now it *must* be time, Grannie."

"It's sure to be four now," says Molly.

"Nine minutes to four," says Grannie. "But, my dears, as you are so anxious for your little neighbour to come, why don't you go and meet him?"

Nothing could give them greater pleasure, and with an air of relief they run away.

They quite expect to meet him in the lane, hurrying towards them. But there is no sign of him there, nor in the drive when they peep through the gate.

They do not squeeze their faces against the bars

as they did this morning, but walk boldly up to the house to call for him.

The hall door is shut and the bell is beyond Molly's reach even when she stands upon the extreme tips of her square toes.

"I can't reach it," she says panting, and with a rosy face, "I shall have to lift you up, Sibyl, and you must give a loud pull. They will know it is us."

Sibyl brings two strong, willing little hands to bear upon the bell, and it rings such a peal that it sounds as if a band of soldiers were insisting upon being admitted.

"They will hear that," says Molly, shaking herself to set herself to rights.

"I pulled it nice and loud, didn't I?" says Sibyl.

In their eagerness to be let in, they press so close against the door that when it is opened suddenly they fall flat upon their faces in the hall. They are helped up at once, and a voice hopes that they have not hurt themselves.

An old man stands before them dressed in black, and with a kind, grave face.

"We came to fetch—" begins Molly, then stops. "Prince Charming," is on the tip of her tongue, but perhaps the old man would not know who is meant. She has forgotten Arthur's surname, and so has Sibyl. Their faces look very blank for an instant, then they brighten as the same thought crosses the mind of each, and they say boldly, the two voices sounding like one,

"We came to fetch our next door neighbour."

The grave butler puts his hand before his mouth to hide a grave smile that creeps over it. But no doubt he has heard about Molly and Sibyl, for he crosses the hall, and leads the way to the drawing-room at once.

"It is just the same furniture as it was when Mr. and Mrs. Bertram lived here," says Sibyl when they are alone.

"It is a furnished house, and that means it is let with the furniture and all," says Molly.

"This is the big arm-chair what dear Mr. Bertram used to sit in," says Sibyl, wriggling herself back into it. "Come and sit by the side of me, sister. It is quite comfy for two."

As they sit side by side, their arms twined lovingly round each other's necks, you can see that though alike in some ways, in others they are very different. Molly's face is so much plumper, and her hair fairer. It waves in fluffy bits of down over a broad white brow, while Sibyl's face is smaller and thinner, and her hair is done up in front in one large curl upon the top of her head, and kept in its place with a hair-pin.

"Do you know, Sibyl," says Molly suddenly, "I've been thinking,—and I am sure Grannie never pays visits without a bonnet on,—we ought to have had on our best bonnets, just as we do when we pay visits with Grannie."

Molly's solemn voice overawes Sibyl. She puts her hand to the top of her head, and pats it dolefully.

"Do you think Arthur will mind?" she says.

"Perhaps he won't," says Molly; "but there is the man who opened the door."

"We didn't mean to pay a real, regular wisit," says Sibyl; "we only came to meet Arthur."

"Yes," replies Molly slowly; "but the man didn't know that."

"He must have thought it wery quare," says Sibyl. "Hadn't you better 'splain about the bonnets, sister?"

"He must have thought we didn't know how to behave," says Molly gravely. "What shall we say to him, Sibyl?"

But Sibyl shakes her head hopelessly, and falls to work to suck her thumb. She does this if she is worried, or sad, or perplexed, and she seems to find great comfort from it.

"Tell him we only looked in," she says.

But Molly takes no notice of this idea.

"I tell you what, Sibyl," she says at last in a

bright voice, "we will ask Prince Charming to explain to the man."

Sibyl takes her thumb out of her mouth with an air of relief, and looks admiringly at Molly.

"That is beautiful. You always do think such lovely things, Molly; you are so clever."

Molly kisses her.

"I am glad I thought of it," she says. "And do you know, I have thought another thought since we have been sitting here?"

"*Have* you?"

"Yes; I am sure we ought not to be both sitting in one chair. I have been to pay visits with Grannie—"

"So have I," says Sibyl hastily; "don't leave me out."

"I won't," says Molly; "only I've been the oftenest, because I am so much older than you. But, Sibyl, when you paid visits, you never saw Grannie and another person sitting in one chair, did you?"

"I don't 'member," replies Sibyl slowly. "You went only two days ago,—don't you 'member for certain, Molly?"

"I'm trying," says Molly thoughtfully. "We went to visit Mr. and Mrs. Strong, and we sat in the sitting-room where the glass thing with the flowers is."

"A 'serva-story," says Sibyl.

Molly nods.

"Grannie did not sit in the same chair with Mrs. Strong, and she didn't sit in the same chair with Mr. Strong, and she didn't sit in the same chair with me, so she must have sat in a chair all by herself."

"Then we will sit in chairs all by ourselves," says Sibyl springing up. "Come 'long, sister, which shall we choose?"

A few seconds later, when Prince Charming enters, instead of the two little girls cuddled cosily back in one arm-chair, he finds them, a great way apart from each other, sitting upon the tallest and straightest chairs the room contains, their toes stuck stiffly out before them, their backs very erect, and their faces trying hard to look as if their best bonnets were not in the wardrobe at home, but where they want them to be—upon the top of their bright little heads.

As Arthur appears, the sisters give a cry of mingled delight and admiration, their stiffness vanishes in an instant; they jump down from their high seats and run forward to greet him.

He has thrown aside his morning suit, and is dressed in an old-fashioned, quaint costume of dark sapphire blue velvet, silk stockings to match, and shoes with sparkling buckles. The dark blue is set off by a falling collar and ruffles of old lace yellow with age, and in his hand he holds a cap to match the velvet, with a buckle to match his shoes set upon one side of it. His cheeks are flushed, his brown eyes bright with excitement, and his lips curve into a happy smile as he sees his two little visitors.

Molly and Sibyl are lost in admiration. What they would like to do would be to throw their four warm arms round his neck and draw him down for a good hug. But he is so much more a Prince Charming now than even he was this morning, and for once shyness steps in and they content themselves with standing still and—looking at him.

"We want to explain something," says Molly, taking his hand and speaking earnestly. "We thought we should meet you in the lane, and we didn't put on our bonnets 'cause we were in a hurry. And we want you to tell the man that this is not a real, regular visit, but we only just *looked in* to fetch you because you were so late."

"And tell him," puts in Sibyl hastily, "that we really and truly do know how to behave ourselves, for Grannie always takes Molly or me when she goes to pay wisits."

"I am sorry I was so late," says Arthur, "and

that you had all the trouble of coming to fetch me."

"Oh, it was not any trouble. We liked it," says Molly, "and perhaps you were not very late, only we were rather early. The clocks wouldn't go after we got ready."

"Don't forget to tell the man," says Sibyl.

"Had I better tell him now?" asks Arthur.

"I think it would be safest," says Molly. "Because you might be sleepy, and forget this evening."

The butler is holding the door open for them. Arthur steps up to him and says a few words in a low voice. Molly and Sibyl stand gravely hand-in-hand, watching the butler's face. He does not even smile, and their dignity is satisfied.

A little while later the drawing-room door at Shadie Cottage is thrown widely open, and Grannie is waked up so suddenly from a nap, that she rubs her eyes and blinks them, wondering if she is dreaming still, for coming towards her is a slender figure with a head covered with yellow curls and earnest brown eyes looking out of it. He is dressed in dark blue and creamy white; and as he advances, two voices cry from the background,

"Grannie, here is Prince Charming."

"Ah! yes! Just for the moment I forgot," says Grannie, sitting upright, and putting on her spectacles to have a better view of her visitor. "I ought to have remembered you were coming, my dear, for Molly and Sibyl have been talking about you the whole day. But old ladies like a nap now and then. And when you came in I was waked up so suddenly that for the moment I could not remember who you were."

"I flung the door open," says Sibyl penitently. "I am so sorry, Grannie."

"Never mind," says Grannie. "And how are you, my dear?" turning to Arthur. "I hear you came down here because you are so delicate."

"Cerisette thinks I am better already, thank you," says Arthur.

"You are very thin, my dear," says Grannie. "I hope you will grow fatter before you go away."

"But he has only just come, Grannie," says Sibyl quickly. "And I want him to live here all his life long."

"And if he lives to be as old as I am that will be a very long time," says Grannie.

"Our Grannie is everybody's Grannie," says Sibyl, "and she is to be yours too, Arthur. You must call her Grannie just as we do, and you will never have another Grannie who will be half as nice."

"Here is Maria with my tea. You don't have yours until by-and-by," says Grannie, "but you can stay and see me eat mine if you like."

"But may we not take him out and show him the garden?" asks Sibyl coaxingly.

"Do as you please, my dears, so that you do not tire Arthur. He is not so strong as you are, and you must have some mercy upon his poor legs."

"I'll take care of him, Grannie," says Molly in a motherly voice, and with Prince Charming between them they pass out into the garden.

CHAPTER VII.

IT IS ALL A'TWEEN US.

AFTER tea the two sisters take Arthur to show him their play-room.

It is a fair-sized, uncarpeted room, with a cupboard built into the wall, a strongly made table, a few chairs, and a large wide sofa, covered with old-fashioned, well-worn chintz. The floor, table, chairs, and sofa are crowded with toys, or rather pieces of toys. You may search the whole room from one end to the other, and I do not believe you will find a single toy that is whole and sound. There are many animals, but not one animal with its own four legs upon its own proper body. Lying down by the sofa is a cow that *seems* quite itself, but if you take it in your hand and examine it, you will find that Sibyl, in her hurry to mend it when Jacob's glue-pot was nice and handy, has put a horse's head upon it instead of its own. There is an odd-looking creature staring down at you from the table. There is a familiar air about it, yet you cannot think *what* animal it is meant to be. It is the body of a donkey with the head of a water-spaniel glued on to it. Sibyl took up the first head that happened to be near her, and as it fitted she put it on. She is very proud of her work, and has great affection for that animal. Sometimes she calls it "my dear dog," sometimes "my dear donkey." One name does as well as the other.

"Nothing belongs to nobody in this room," says Sibyl in a lordly voice, and waving her hands about as she stands by Arthur's side. "Nothing belongs to nobody here. It is all a'tween us."

Such a wistful look comes into Arthur's brown

eyes and curves the corners of his mouth. This is just what he has missed all his life long. Everything has always been his very own. Nothing has ever been "a'tween us." Think what it would be to live alone in the world, and have no one to share things with us. We cannot enjoy anything alone. If it is only a book we read or a thought we think, how naturally we turn to talk it over with a friend we love, or of whose sympathy we are sure. And as our pleasures are double if we share them, so our sorrows are only half sorrows if we can tell them and be comforted. A great deal of mischief is done every day by the bad habit of brooding over things when we are alone. Perhaps some one is a little unkind to us, and we sit down and brood over it. We wrap it up and keep it to ourselves, and bit by bit it grows, until at last, like the cloud which was at first no bigger than a man's hand, it fills the whole of our world and is the means of separating us from some one who is very dear to us. And just in the same way Arthur had brooded about his father, and thought, when he was absent, only of the time when he would come again, so that he had become the sad and spiritless little boy he was when we saw him in his London home. There is no sadder person than the Miller of the Dee—if he ever lived—and he, you know, is proud of saying,

> "I care for nobody, no, not I,
> And nobody cares for me."

And I am not sure but that loving one person, only one person, with a very exclusive love, is not quite as bad as the Miller of the Dee, who cared "for nobody." It is no wonder, is it, that if he cares for nobody, nobody cares for him?

And a great longing is stirred in Arthur's heart as his wistful brown eyes glance over the broken toys and rest upon the happy pair of sisters. He does not clearly understand where the difference lies, but he only knows that he is yearning to share his treasures with them, not only his toys, but some of the love that the good GOD has given to all of us, and which has waked up in Arthur at that tiny speech of Sibyl's, "it is all a'tween us."

So the little fellow, who is usually so sober and quiet, stretches out his arms as if he would embrace the whole room full of broken toys, and cries with quivering lips and big tears springing into his brown eyes,

"Oh, please may I bring my toys here,—and *may* they be all between us ? Please, *please* let me bring them."

"Oh, yes," answers Molly in a matter-of-fact surprised voice; "you can bring as many of your toys as you like. There is plenty of room."

"Oh, plenty of room. Bring them all, every one of them," says Sibyl gleefully. "I 'spect they are great beauties. When will you bring them, Arthur?"

"To-morrow," says Arthur, sobering down into his quiet self once more.

"That will be *wery* nice," says Sibyl in a satisfied voice. "But what makes your face so wery red, Prince Charming? Is the room too hot? but I am 'fraid there isn't another window we can open."

Half-an-hour later, when Uncle Edward looks in, he finds the party of three quite at home. Prince Charming is sitting upon the ground, his velvet suit and silk stockings soiled and dusty, while Molly upon one side of him, and Sibyl upon the other, each with an arm twined lovingly round his neck, are kissing and hugging him to their hearts' content.

"You are choking your visitor," is Uncle Edward's greeting, as the sisters pounce upon him.

"No,. oh no," says Sibyl in a shocked voice; "we have given him a good tea, and now we are amoosing him. Come and help amoose him, Uncle Edward."

"Sit down upon the sofa," says Molly, upsetting the toys to make way for him.

"It's old, but it's wery comfy," says Sibyl, doing the honours of their furniture.

"You need not introduce me to this sofa," says Uncle Edward, sitting upon it and leaning back; "I knew it when I was a baby,—this sofa and I have been friends for nearly forty years."

"Oh, Uncle," cries Sibyl, "why how is it your hair isn't white?"

"I had no idea you were so old," says Molly putting her head upon one side and regarding him with fresh interest.

"Then perhaps you will listen to me with greater respect," says Uncle Edward, "for I have a complaint to make. Prepare yourselves for a trial, and let me see if you are innocent or guilty."

The two sisters stand very upright before Uncle Edward; they clasp their hands behind their backs, their faces trying to keep grave, but little dimples peep out and play hide-and-seek every now and then.

"We are going to be tried," explains Sibyl to Arthur; "but don't cry, 'cause it's only make-believe."

"Uncle Edward is the judge, and we are the prisoners," says Molly.

"I wish you were a little more sorry," says Uncle Edward. "Do you know what you have done?"

"No," says Molly.

"No," says Sibyl.

"Then are you innocent, or guilty?"

"Innocent," cry the two voices.

"When I came home this evening," says Uncle Edward, "I went to my room to dress for dinner; I took off my coat, and walked to the wash-hand stand to plunge my face into a basin of water—".

"That was wery bad for you if you was hot," interrupts Sibyl, shaking her head. "Maria says so,—it will make your face *spotty*."

"The water was not cold but lukewarm, which makes all the difference," says Uncle Edward. "Before I dipped my face I stretched out my hand for a sponge,—there was no sponge. That was 'quare,' as Sibyl would say, but it was 'quarer' still when I found that nail-brushes, tooth-brush, in fact every one of my things had vanished as if a conjuror had whisked them away."

The sisters' faces dimple with delight. Molly claps her hands, and says gleefully,

"*Of course* you couldn't find them, because we have been tidying up for you. Grannie likes us to tidy up."

"Yes, and your room was in *such* a litter," says Sibyl reprovingly. "It wanted tidying up dreadful,—and we had nothing else to do. It looked *lovely* when we left it."

"After a long hunt I found my nail-brushes, tooth-brush, and sponges where I least expected to find them—in the drawer with my clean shirts. One of my hair-brushes was upon the top shelf in the wardrobe—"

"We threw it up," says Sibyl. "It tumbled down a great many times, the stupid thing, but it stayed up at last."

"The other brush I found inside one of my best boots—"

"It fitted in so nicely," says Molly, "and there was no room for it anywhere else."

"The boots themselves I found in the wardrobe underneath my dress coat, and my slippers lay upon the top of my collars and cuffs. My nail-scissors I found in the box where I keep my diamond studs—"

"They was lovely," says Sibyl, delightedly. "They shined like stars. Molly and me tried them on, and we wondered why you never wear them when you are here."

"Now, you must listen and be serious," says Uncle Edward, putting one hand on the shoulder of each of them and drawing them to him. "I cannot allow you to go into my room at all if you do not promise me that you will not tidy up—as you call it—again. You can tidy up your own rooms as much as you please. I am sure this room, for instance, wants tidying up if ever a room did, and you can begin upon it to-morrow morning."

"Oh, but that would never do," cries Molly, with a blank face. "We can never find anything when it is tidy. Can we, sister?"

"No, never!" cries Sibyl. "Oh, we don't like the room tidy *at all*, Uncle Edward."

"Ah! That is just the case with me. I can never find anything when *my* room is tidy, so I hope you will remember the golden rule, and 'do unto others as you would they should do unto you!' Now what are you going to say?" and Uncle Edward releases them from his grasp.

"We are very sorry," says Molly, her roguish blue eyes looking her uncle straight in the face.

"We will never do so no more," says Sibyl, rolling her pinafore in her hands and poking one of her shoulders nearly up to her ears.

"We hope you will forgive us," says Molly.

"And we give you a thousand kisses," says Sibyl, springing upon him, and Molly follows her example; their four arms clasped tightly round his neck while kisses rain down upon his cheeks, forehead, nose, moustaches, hair, and some of them even fall upon the back of his coat.

"And how have they been 'amoosing' you, Prince Charming?" asks Uncle Edward, when he has breath enough to speak.

"They have shown me the garden and their play-room, and I have been very happy, thank you," says Arthur, shyly. "And Molly says I may bring my toys here, and we can have them all between us. Will not that be nice?" and his brown eyes brighten as he looks to Uncle Edward for sympathy.

"Very nice indeed if you don't mind having them broken," says Uncle Edward, shrugging his shoulders and sweeping a glance around him. "Where is that china tea-set I brought you from London, Molly, about ten days ago? Not a piece of it left to tell the tale, I suppose."

"Oh, yes," replies Molly with pride, "we have

been *very* careful over it, and have only had it out now and then. There is only the sugar-basin broken, and the lid of the tea-pot, and a few cups, and saucers, and plates. Grannie is going to join them together with some stuff that mends china beautiful. She will mend your china and make it as good as new, Uncle Edward."

"Thank you," says Uncle Edward. "But as I have no little nieces living up in London with me, my china does not want joining. And how about the doll I brought you, Sibyl, the same time I brought Molly the tea-set."

"She is as good as new," says Sibyl cheerfully. "She broke her two legs and her two arms, but Molly put her on two fresh legs and two fresh arms, and then her head fell off and I put her on Lady Mildred's head, because Lady Mildred had lost her body, and now she is *quite* as good as new. Would you like to see her, Uncle Edward?"

"No, thank you," says her uncle drily. "By-the-bye, children, I had a letter by the morning's post which I did not read until after breakfast, and then I found in it a great piece all about Prince Charming."

"Oh," cries Sibyl, dropping an armful of toys with a loud clatter upon the floor. "*Do* let us hear it. *Do* tell us about it;" while Molly just as eager presses close against her uncle's knees, and peeps over his shoulder.

"*You* cannot read it, little woman," he says, "but when I have found the place I will read it to you. Here it is. Dr. Courtney writes: 'I have sent down to be your next door neighbour a delicate little fellow called Arthur Adair. I was his father's fag when we were at school together, and even now I remember how easy my fagging was when compared with that of the other fellows. We did not meet, after we left school, until a few weeks ago, when we came across each other's path, and found out we had been old schoolfellows. He told me about his only son, how many doctors had seen him, and how little better he seemed to get, and he asked me to look in upon him one day. I did so, and luckily thought of the empty house next door I saw when I was staying with you. It is not country air he wants so much as bright companions to cheer him and interest him, and those two little nieces of yours will be the very best medicine for him.'"

"Oh," cries Arthur eagerly. "Then that was what the doctor meant," and he explains to the three the mystery about the strange medicine he was to find at Riverside.

"How quare," says Sibyl thoughtfully, "for Molly and me to be two bottles of medicine. But we are wery nice medicine, arn't we, Prince Charming?"

"Very nice indeed," says Arthur.

"Now I will finish about it," says Uncle Edward, reading from the letter. "'Will you ask your mother if she will be so kind as to call and let him see as much of Molly and Sibyl as she thinks fit? I know her kind heart, and I do not hesitate to ask her this. Molly and Sibyl will work wonders, and under their care, I expect to find my little patient in a few weeks quite bonny and bright. I have only seen him once, but he struck me as being a very sweet little fellow, and your nieces—'"

"There," says Uncle Edward, as he folds up the letter rather hastily. "That is all I need read. The rest does not concern you—much."

"But it was about us," says Molly suspiciously. "You did not finish about us. We want to know what more Dr. Courtney said about us."

"It is sure to be something wery nice," says Sibyl, "for he was a wery nice man. Do read it, please, Uncle Edward," (very coaxingly.)

"Not a word more," replies their uncle, putting the letter into his pocket-book. "Dr. Courtney little thinks you made your next door neighbour's acquaintance so soon."

"Why of *course*," says Molly serenely, "Grannie says it is only neighbourly to call upon your next door neighbour."

"But you did not wait for Grannie," says Uncle Edward. "And I must say you have what Sibyl calls a 'quare' way of managing your affairs down here. When we want to know our neighbours in London we do not climb up ladders and sit upon the top of a wall to see them come out of their house."

"The wall was too high for us to peep over, and we were obliged to climb up the ladders," says Molly.

But the faces of the sisters grow very red as they call to mind their visit this afternoon without their bonnets. What would their uncle say to *that?* He would be quite sure that people in London would never pay visits with bare heads and without being properly dressed.

"But it wasn't a real, regular wisit," says Sibyl in a comforting whisper, as they gaze into each other's startled eyes. "It was only *looking in.*"

"That was all," Molly whispers softly back.

Uncle Edward is talking to Prince Charming,

and does not hear the whisper. Arthur's eyes shone, while he listened to the letter, and now they are lighting up with a new interest as he forgets his shyness, and puts his hand upon Uncle Edward's coat-sleeve.

"I am so glad that the nice doctor knew Father when he was a boy like me," he says softly. "Do you think I shall ever see him again to ask him what Father did and all about him?"

"I am sure you will," answers Uncle Edward, "for I fancy from what Dr. Courtney says that he and your father are getting firm friends. And if you stay here long enough you will see him, for he often runs down for a couple of days' rest. He is a great friend of mine."

"Only stays long enough," quotes Sibyl bristling. "Why, Prince Charming is not going away never no more. Grannie is his Grannie, and you are his Uncle Edward, and Molly and me are his sisters, and these toys—" waving her hand—"are all to be a'tween him as well as a'tween Molly and me."

"As for the toys, I don't think much of that part of the bargain," says Uncle Edward. "What do *you* say, Prince Charming?"

Arthur colours brightly.

"It is *so* nice," he says, "because they are to be between us. I have had my toys to myself, and I do not care for them a bit. But you are so kind to me," and to the children's great surprise he lays his head down upon Uncle Edward's shoulder and sobs.

"Why he must have hurt himself," says Sibyl. "I'll run and ask Grannie for some sticking-plaster. Don't cry, *dear* Arthur."

"Kiss the place and make it well," says Molly soothingly.

"Let him alone," says Uncle Edward, who understands all about it now. "He will be quite himself soon. Let him cry in peace."

"I am crying because I am so happy," says Arthur between his sobs.

"Now how wery quare of you, Prince Charming,"

says Sibyl. "Molly and me only cry when we arn't happy or when we have hurt ourselves."

"Never mind," says Molly. "He will be himself soon, Uncle Edward says so. Don't cry, Prince Charming—no, *do* cry, I mean, if it does you good," and she pats his yellow curls with quite a motherly touch. "We love him very much indeed, don't we, sister?"

"Wery, wery much," replies Sibyl, and they each of them press a grave kiss upon the back of his neck and stand quietly hand-in-hand beside him until his tears have stopped.

CHAPTER VIII.

UNDER THREE UMBRELLAS.

THE beautiful summer days pass like a dream to the three happy children,—Molly, Sibyl, and Arthur. They are always together,—either Arthur is with them at Shadie Cottage, or they are with him at Riverside.

Cerisette has grown used to the sisters and their odd ways. At first she was really afraid they would lead Arthur into danger—break his neck, or something. But by degrees she learnt to trust them, and now she has become quite fond of the "English little ladies," as she calls them.

Arthur is not rosy or plump, I do not suppose

he will ever be either of those things, even if he lives to be a big man, but he is quite different to what he was when first he came to Riverside. There is a touch of healthy colour in his cheeks, his eyes are bright, he runs about and plays, and laughs, and does not get sleepy until the evening; and then, as all children know, the dustman goes round and throws dust into their eyes, and they are obliged to feel sleepy whether they wish it or no.

Arthur's toys have been carried into the playroom at Shadie Cottage, and it need hardly be said, there is not a whole one left. The carved ivory animals from the large Noah's ark are only fit for the doctor. The rein-deer lies upon the floor, a front leg missing and a slender horn broken off; the elephant's trunk is in two pieces; a cow has lost a tail; a horse's head is in a corner, its body somewhere else; a squirrel is looking in vain for the nut he was cracking; and a splendid Newfoundland dog has only one ear. But then, as

Sibyl carefully explains to Arthur, "You cannot find out how to join things together unless they are broken," and Arthur is so happy that the destruction of his toys does not trouble him, though he is, by nature, a most careful little man, and his things are just as whole and nice when he has finished with them as when they first came into his possession.

"Arthur," says Sibyl one day, turning suddenly to him, "why is it that when your papa goes away, you run to your bedroom, and shut your door tight, and won't come to play with Molly and me for a wery long time?"

"I am always so sorry when Father goes away," says Arthur; "but I know it vexes him to see me cry, so I wait until he has gone, and then I shut myself in my room and have a good cry. But Father is coming next week to stay here for his holiday, and that *will* be nice."

"It is wery quare about your crying," says Sibyl, looking at him with a puzzled expression. "Molly and me *could* cry sometimes when somebody wery nice goes away, but we couldn't cry *after* they had gone. We shouldn't have time."

"Should not you?" says Arthur meekly. "But then I have plenty of time,—I have not so much to do as you and Molly."

"That is wery true," says Sibyl. "Now, this afternoon you must come with us, Prince Charming. We are going to see whether Mrs. Grey's chickens are hatched, and if Nannie Straw is better, and oh! a great many other things. Molly has written them down upon a piece of paper, as long as that, in small writing. Molly's small writing is *wery* clever,—nobody else can read it 'cept herself. You can't, can you, Arthur?"

"No," answers Arthur; "I tried the other day, and found I could not."

"Here she is," says Sibyl, as Molly comes towards them, a piece of paper in one hand, a pencil in the other, and with altogether an air of business about her.

"I was wondering where you both were," she says. "We shall have to start directly after dinner, and we shall not be home until tea-time. You must put on your biggest hat, Arthur, and please bring an umbrella, because it is so hot."

"Oh, I don't want an umbrella," pleads Arthur, "I really don't."

"Oh yes, you do," says Molly briskly. "We are all going to take umbrellas to-day,—Sibyl is to have Grannie's, I shall have Uncle Edward's, and you can have one of your papa's. Parasols are no use with a hot sun,—Grannie said so to Maria the other day, when Maria wanted her to take the little parasol with the lace round. Grannie said, 'That is only for show, Maria; I want something that will be of use to-day. Bring me my umbrella, please.'"

And Arthur says nothing, but meekly submits. Molly always has her own way with him.

Early in the afternoon they start, and they take up the whole width of the lane from hedge to hedge, as they walk along. Grannie's umbrella nearly covers Sibyl from head to foot, as she leans it upon her shoulders; you can only see a pair of little black socks and boots pattering underneath it. Uncle Edward's umbrella is larger still, and Molly is borne down by the weight of it. No socks are seen in her case, only a pair of boots. Arthur's slender figure staggers under the weight of his—an old one of his father's—but he is taller than Molly, so that a good piece of white sailor trousers is showing as he trudges on.

They walk slowly for some distance, but their arms ache, and they feel unusually tired. The umbrellas are woefully heavy, but neither of them likes to be the first to complain.

By-and-by Sibyl's umbrella shuts with a loud snap, and she falls down, her head and shoulders folded up in it. She screams with fright, and Molly and Arthur rush at once to pick her up and get the umbrella away from her. It takes some time to comfort her, but her tears are dried at last;

then they make another start, but she insists upon changing umbrellas with Molly first.

Their spirits are better after the rest they have had, and as Sibyl sees a tomtit sitting in the hedge, she makes a dart at it. But she forgets her umbrella, which is so heavy that it tilts her forward. She catches hold of Molly to save herself, but Molly has no hands to spare, and both the sisters roll over into the ditch, their big umbrellas floating upon the top of them.

Arthur has to be comforter alone this time, and sets to his work like a man. The two sisters are scratched and bruised. Sibyl howls bitterly—but Molly manages, by winking very hard, not to shed a tear. They can only find two handkerchiefs between the three, and these have to be used to dry Sibyl's tears and to wipe the dust from hands, and knees, and faces. And, as you may fancy, Molly and Sibyl do not look much like paying visits this afternoon.

Still they persevere for some distance yet with

the umbrellas. It is Sibyl who is the one to give up. She suddenly plants her umbrella upright upon its stick—there it stands, a big, black mushroom in the middle of the white road—and stretching out her tired arms, she says decidedly,

"I am not going to carry that nasty thing any further, Molly."

"But we cannot leave Uncle Edward's umbrella in the middle of the road for anybody to pick up. He would be vexed with us, and have to buy a new one," says Molly, soberly.

"If we shut them they will not be so heavy, and then they will not make our arms ache," says Arthur, brightly.

"Let us try," says Molly. And so they do, and find the plan much better.

At the first house at which they call Sibyl leaves her umbrella behind her. Molly does not find this out for some time, but when she does, she insists that they must go all the way back and fetch it.

By this time it occurs to Molly that they had

better put off their visiting till another day. She mentions it to the others, who agree with her joyfully.

But they return in quite a different style to that in which they started. They are footsore and weary, and their arms ache sadly. Their frocks are dusty, their faces, legs, and hands scratched and bruised, and they drag heavily after them three shut-up umbrellas.

The two sisters are so fretful that night, so much more tired and sleepy than usual, that Maria wonders what they have been doing, and questions them closely about their scratches and bruises. But they will not tell her.

And when next they go to pay visits, whether in the village or with Grannie, they leave their umbrellas at home. Molly too is heard to say to Arthur the next day in a meek voice,

"You were quite right, Arthur, about the umbrellas. It would have been better not to have taken them."

CHAPTER IX.

GRANNIE REFUSES TO BE NEIGHBOURLY.

ABOUT the end of September something happens which throws Molly and Sibyl into the wildest state of excitement. You will remember if you go back to the second chapter that I described three houses lying side by side, and one of these is called the Red House. It is large and rather gloomy, for it is very much shut in by trees and shrubs, and it is built of red brick, from whence it gets its name.

It is three years since the two little sisters came to live with Grannie, and all that long time the Red House has been empty, with no one living in it. Many people have *looked* at it, but nobody has ever yet taken it. Some say that it is too large, others that it is too dull, and so on.

"We have never had no next door neighbours here," Sibyl explains to Arthur, waving her hand towards the high, close hedge which separates them from the Red House. "It would be very nice if we had you know, 'cause they could look out of the windows and see a great deal of us."

"The windows are some way off," says Arthur. "What a big house it is. You count the chimneys, Sibyl. What a number there are."

"I don't think I could count so many," says Sibyl. "It is a wery big house, and Molly and me always want to go inside, but they keep the gate locked so tight, and we never can get in. Shouldn't you like to see inside it?"

"No, I do not think I care much about it," answers Arthur, slowly.

"You are a wery quare little boy, Prince Charming," says Sibyl, thoughtfully. "But Grannie says you are a wery *good* little boy, and she says she wishes all day long that Molly and me was as good as you. But we arn't *wery* good. We are always doing naughty things, and then we are sorry after we have done them."

"I am not good," says Arthur, blushing rosy red, and a pained look coming into his sweet brown eyes. "Indeed I am not good, Sibyl. *Really* and truly I am not."

"Oh, yes, you are," says Sibyl, positively. "I watch you in church on Sunday and you shut your eyes wery tight, and say your prayers wery hard, and sing your hymns wery loud. Arthur," —and Sibyl draws closer to him and tucks her hand into his arm,—"don't the flies worry you in church? Don't they come and sit on the end of your nose and *tickle* you?"

"No," says Arthur, "I don't think they do. At least I don't feel them."

"That is wery quare," says Sibyl, "'cause they do worry Molly and me. There is one fly with a blue tip to his tail—I know him wery well indeed —and he *always* will come and sit upon the end of my nose in church. He has come every summer since we've been at Grannie's. I think he is a wery rude fly, for I don't want him to come, and Molly doesn't either. He must be getting wery old now. Perhaps,"—very hopefully,—" perhaps he'll die soon. Flies do die, Arthur, don't they? They don't turn into butterflies, like those things Grannie was telling us about?"

" Oh, no," says Arthur. " It is only the chrysalis that turns into a butterfly. I have a book in London with coloured pictures in it, and all of different butterflies and the chrysalis they come from. I'll ask Father to bring it when he goes up to London for the day. He is going next week I think."

" It is not a wery 'tickler book, is it?" asks Sibyl, wistfully. " Not one you've got to be wery careful over, and wash your hands every time you read it? 'Cause if it is, perhaps it had better stay in its own home in London, and your papa had better not bring it down here."

"Father says it is a valuable book," answers Arthur. "But I am sure he would like you to see it, and I do not mind anything that you and Molly do to it."

"That is wery kind of you, dear Arthur," replies Sibyl. "You *are* wery kind, you know. Grannie says it is so kind of you to threadle her needles for her, 'cause she is old, and she can't see to threadle them for herself."

"Oh, but it is so nice to do anything for Grannie," says Arthur, eagerly. "I like to thread her needles, I do indeed."

"Molly and me don't, 'cause we have to sit so still," says Sibyl. "And now Molly says that 'cause you have done it, when you are in your own house we shall have to threadle them for Grannie. We shall take it in turns. First Molly and then me."

"We will run in now and see if she wants

any threaded before I go in to dinner," says Arthur.

"I wonder if Molly has done the copy Uncle Edward set her," says Sibyl, as they saunter slowly up the rose path. "She is writing your name in big letters all down the page. Not your real name, but the name Uncle Edward gave you,—Prince Charming. And I have learnt to spell it, Grannie teached me. Just hear me spell it. P-r-i-n-c-e Prince, C-h-a-r-m-i-n-g, Charming, Prince Charming. Oh, here is Molly. She has finished writing your name, and she has come to show us how she has written it."

It is just as the leaves are pulling off their green coats and putting on their red and yellow ones that this wonderful something happens. The Red House is no longer to be let. Somebody has taken it.

This is a good time for Molly and Sibyl, for they are nearly wild with excitement. Every day they bring in a fresh piece of news, and their little tongues go so fast, that Grannie says they are like the clapper of a bell. The only drawback to their happiness is that they cannot rouse Arthur to be in the least excited or disturbed about the wonderful tidings. He is so very quiet, and evidently cares very little about it, though for the sisters' sake he tries to listen and be interested in all they have to tell him.

One van-load of furniture arrives at the Red House. The gates swing wide open, and the huge van creaks and groans as it plunges heavily in at them. Then the gates shut after it. This is only the beginning of the amusement; more furniture must come, and then the neighbours themselves! So Molly and Sibyl think, and they wait upon the tip-toe of expectation. But,—and this is the funniest part of the affair,—*nothing else happens*. The van comes out, after the furniture has been unloaded, and the gates shut after it again, and that is all. Days pass, two weeks have passed, and no person and no things have been seen to go in or out of the gates of the Red House.

And yet there must be *some one* there. All the people are agreed about that. For every now and then the white smoke curls gaily upwards from the chimneys of the Red House. And we know there is no smoke without fire, and fire cannot be lighted without hands. So there is a person or persons at the Red House, but who or what they are nobody can tell.

Molly and Sibyl are as curious as it is possible for two little people to be. They never appear from a walk without some fresh story about " our next door neighbours," each wilder than the last. These are a few of them.

1. "The Red House is taken by a gentleman whose arms and legs were *all* shot off in battle. He never leaves his room, but has a faithful attendant who wheels him up and down it in a wheel chair.

2. "The Red House is taken by a gentleman

who is fond of keeping wild animals about him. He has four tigers, two leopards, one lion, and two panthers. They are very dangerous, and that is why he does not wish for visitors.

3. "The Red House is taken by a lady who is melancholy. She sits upon the sofa all the day and plays a guitar.

4. "The Red House is taken by a lady who has twenty-five cats. Each cat has a separate room, and a little bed lined with red, or pink, or blue, or yellow satin. And each cat has its own silver plate, knife, fork, and spoon."

Even Arthur is roused to some curiosity, especially about the gentleman who owns the wild animals. *If* it is true, he says, he should like to know the gentleman and the animals.

But Molly and Sibyl wait pretty quietly upon the whole. They feel so sure of seeing inside the Red House and becoming acquainted with their neighbours. Grannie always call upon her neighbours, for Grannie likes to be neighbourly, and *of course* she will call upon the people at the Red House after she has waited for them to shake down in their new house. Grannie says it is not kind to call upon your neighbours until you have given them time to shake down. This is what the sisters tell each other over and over again.

There is one thing that troubles them. When they go to pay visits with Grannie they only go one at a time. And which of them is to be the one to pay this particular visit? It is Sibyl's turn, but Molly is the eldest. They end their dispute by agreeing to ask Grannie to take them both. Grannie is so kind she always says "yes" when she can, and there is no reason why she cannot say "yes" in this case.

The people at the Red House have had plenty of time to shake down, and Grannie says never a word about calling upon them. She listens with a smile to the many stories the children pour into her ears, but she never says, as they are always expecting she will, "My dears, ask Maria to dress one of you to pay a visit with me this afternoon. I am going to call upon our neighbours at the Red House."

"Do you think Grannie has forgotten?" asks Sibyl of Molly.

"She can't have forgotten," says Molly, "because we are always talking about them."

"So we are," says Sibyl with a sigh.

"But perhaps we had better remind Grannie," says Molly, "for I heard Maria say the other day that when people are old the time goes so quickly that they don't quite remember how it goes."

"And perhaps Grannie supposes that it is only a few days instead of a long, long while," says Sibyl brightly.

"That is it, you may depend upon it," says Molly, nodding wisely. "And we will tell her this very day when we go to say good-night to her."

And in the soft, subdued light of the candles two little figures stand that same evening, hand-in-hand before Grannie, waiting to speak to her.

"Now, my dears, I really think you get later and later every day," says Grannie's gentle voice. "You must say your Psalm, and go to bed at once."

"We have got something to tell you first, Grannie," says Sibyl eagerly.

"Very well, my dear, what is it?" asks Grannie.

"We think, Grannie, that our next door neighbours have had plenty of time to shake down by now," says Molly.

"Yes, my love, plenty of time," says Grannie quietly. "Why Arthur must have been here—let me see, how many months? You ought to know better than I."

"Oh, Grannie, we don't mean Prince Charming," breaks in Sibyl. "We mean our other side neighbours."

"The people at the Red House," says Molly.

"Yes, my dears," says Grannie wonderingly; "but what have we to do with the people at the Red House? It does not matter to us whether they have shaken down or not, does it?"

"Oh yes, Grannie," says Sibyl, poking one shoulder nearly up to her ears in her eagerness; "it does matter a wery great deal, 'cause when they have shaken down, you are going to call."

Grannie carefully places her spectacles upon her nose, then turns them upon the excited children.

"Who has been putting such nonsense into your heads, my dears?" she says. "I never meant to call upon the people at the Red House."

"Grannie!!!!" shrieks Sibyl.

"Grannie!!!" shrieks Molly.

"Why, my loves, what have I said? What *is* the matter?" cries Grannie in a quavering voice. "You can't both be taken ill at the same moment surely? What *is* the matter?"

"Grannie," gasps Molly, "you always said you liked to be neighbourly!"

"Oh dear, oh dear," howls Sibyl, sitting down upon the floor, and wringing her hands; "now we shall never see the lady who plays upon the cats, nor the gentleman without arms and legs who takes care of the wild animals—"

"No, no, Sibyl," interrupts Molly, "you have it wrong. It is the lady who plays upon the guitar, and another gentleman, not the one, without arms or legs, who looks after the wild animals."

"I don't care," howls Sibyl recklessly, "for if Grannie won't call, we shall never see nothing of anything. Oh, Grannie," in very coaxing tones, "why won't you call? Grannie dear, *do* call."

"Yes, please, dear Grannie," pleads Molly. "You know you always said you liked to be neighbourly, and we *do* want to go with you."

"My dears, if Sibyl will leave off howling, and you will explain," says Grannie; "but at present, if strangers came in they would think I had been beating you. What is all this grief about?"

"We would tell them that you never beat us, dear Grannie," says Molly in a comforting voice; "and we would tell them what a kind, good Grannie you are. Sibyl is crying because we thought you

K

meant to call upon the people at the Red House when they had shaken down. You always like to be neighbourly, don't you, Grannie? And we promised we would tell Arthur all about it, and he will be so sorry, and we are so sorry, and you didn't mean what you said, did you, Grannie dear? and you will call some time, won't you? We don't care how long we wait, so that you call *some time*."

Molly stops to take breath.

"I understand now," says Grannie, "and it is my turn to explain. You are quite right, Molly, I *do* like to be neighbourly, but then all the people we visit I have known something about before, or I have been asked to call. At any rate I have known they would like me to call upon them before I have done so. But the Red House is quite a different matter. We know nothing about the person or people living there,—not even their *name*. My dears, you cannot think I would call upon people when I don't even know their name! Even you must see how impossible it is."

"Oh, but you could find out their name, Grannie," says Sibyl.

"And we want so much to go," coaxes Molly.

"He's got no arms or legs, Grannie," cries Sibyl.

"She sits upon a sofa and plays music," says Molly.

"He keeps wild animals, and Arthur *does* so want to see them."

"My dears, I hope you do not believe all this gossip," says Grannie gently. "My opinion is that the Red House is taken by some people who have trouble or sickness in the family, and who are come down here for perfect rest and quiet. I would not intrude upon them for the world, even if there was no other reason. Why, my loves, we don't know that the people at the Red House want to see us. Indeed I think it is most likely they do *not*."

"Oh, Grannie!" cries Molly, "not want to see you in your nice white cap, and pretty white shawl, and looking so lovely as you always do! Why the

Queen would like to see you! Sibyl and me often wonder why you don't go up to London to visit the Queen."

"Yes we do," exclaims Sibyl. "We are sure she would like wery much to see you."

"And I think the people at the Red House would like *us*," says Molly, "though we are not so beautiful as you, Grannie. Prince Charming says he loves us."

"Wery much indeed," says Sibyl. "Next to his papa. And all the other people they loves us too."

"I am sure they do," says Grannie, taking off her spectacles and winking away a tear that has somehow found its way into the corner of one of her soft blue eyes, "and your old Grannie loves you best of all. But, my dears, you must trust Grannie as well as love her; and you must believe that I do not wish to be unkind when I tell you it is impossible that I should call upon the people at the Red House. Don't think about it, and don't listen to the gossip people talk, but be good and happy with those who love you. I am very glad you have such a nice neighbour as your friend Prince Charming, but you would not find another Prince Charming at the Red House,—they do not drop from the skies every day. Now, trust Grannie, and be good little girls."

Molly and Sibyl do not answer. They say their Psalm in meek voices, give dear Grannie two subdued kisses, and walk hand-in-hand out of the room, with heads hanging down and steps slow. At the bottom of the stairs they stop, and look blankly into each other's eyes.

"I am so wery 'tonished!" says Sibyl shaking her head.

"So am I," replies Molly sorrowfully. "I always thought dear Grannie was so *very* neighbourly."

CHAPTER X.

FROM THE HOLE IN THE HEDGE.

SNIP, snip, snip, snip, snap.

Snip, snip, snip, snip, snap.

Snip,—snip,—sn . . ip,—sn . . ip,—sn . . ap.

"Oh, Sibyl, these garden scissors of Jacob's are so heavy. They hurt my hands."

"It is my turn now, sister. I am not a bit tired," says Sibyl.

"That is because you have not tried them," answers Molly. "They are dreadfully big and heavy; and I don't think you had better try them, Sibyl."

"Just a weeny bit," coaxes Sibyl.

"Very well, but if they hurt you, you must leave off at once," and Molly gives into Sibyl's tiny hands a pair of large garden shears.

I am sorry to say these two little sisters have not followed Grannie's good advice. They wait patiently for a few days, hoping Grannie may change her mind; that she may be asked to call upon the people at the Red House, or that something may turn up. But nothing has turned up. The reports in the village are wilder than ever, and the Red House itself is as silent as it can be. No one is seen to go out or come in, the only sound heard is the cawing of the rooks; nothing stirs except the trees, and the only sign of life is the fleecy white smoke that sometimes curls out of the red-tiled chimneys.

Molly and Sibyl have tried to sit upon the top of the hedge, as they sat upon the top of the wall, but they have failed. They could not get the ladder to stand steady. "It wobbles very much," said Molly, and the first step she took the ladder was nearly on the top of her. So now they are trying to make a large hole at the bottom of the hedge, a hole large enough and wide enough for them to see through it.

It is no easy task, for the quickset hedge is thick and broad, and there are a great many twigs and branches to break off. It requires a good deal of patience and willing fingers. Jacob is in the town to-day buying some seeds, and while he is away they have borrowed his garden shears, and are hard at work, busy as bees.

"They *do* hurt my hands, Molly," says Sibyl after a few minutes, "I would rather break off the sticks with my fingers, and you can have these scissors."

"I thought they would; and now I am rested I can go on again," says Molly. "Jacob must have had these scissors made on purpose for his own hands."

"Jacob's hands are not lily-white, are they?" asks Sibyl thoughtfully. "I heard Uncle Edward read some po'try to Grannie about 'lily-white hands' the other day."

"Jacob's are not, but Prince Charming's are," replies Molly.

"Oh, but then he is lovely altogether," says Sibyl, "and—"

"Do you know," interrupts Molly, "I believe we can see through! It is such a large hole."

"Oh, sister dear," says Sibyl in a most coaxing voice, "let me have the first peep, *please*. I have worked so hard, and I've torn a piece of skin off one of my fingers with a nasty thorn,—a *real* bit of skin, Molly dear," and Sibyl holds out her finger with a piteous air.

"Don't cry!" says Molly quickly. "If you don't cry, you shall have first peep. You must push into the hedge as far as you can get, and lie quite flat or you will scratch your face."

Sibyl does not need to be told twice. She scrambles into the hedge, squeezes her white chin into the earth, and stays quite still while she—looks.

"What do you see?" asks Molly.

"Nothing," calls back a *very* disappointed voice; "only some gravel, and nothing else."

"It is my turn now," says Molly.

But she too sees—nothing.

Then Sibyl tries again. She has not been long in the hole this time before she gives a little shriek, which brings Molly down upon her hands and knees as close as she can get to her sister.

"Oh, Sibyl, what *do* you see?"

"One boot—no—*two* boots," answers Sibyl.

"Are they boots hung out to dry, or are they boots with feet in them? Why did you say *boots?* Are they feet? Be quick, Sibyl."

"They are walking," cries Sibyl. "Now they are walking faster, now they are out of sight, and *oh*, Molly!"

"What else do you see? Be quick, Sibyl, tell me quick," says Molly, excitedly.

Sibyl backs out of the hole and faces Molly.

There is a bright astonished look in her large dark eyes.

"Oh, Molly, I saw *two furry legs*."

"Besides the boots?" asks Molly.

"Yes, besides the boots," says Sibyl.

"I'll look too," says Molly, but she is unlucky, and sees nothing.

"Do you know, sister," says Sibyl, in a hushed voice, "who has come to be our next door neighbour?"

"No," answers Molly.

"Don't you guess?"

"I can't," says Molly, "oh *do* tell me, Sibyl."

"It is somebody out of a fairy story. It is Beauty and the Beast!"

"Oh, but it couldn't be," says Molly.

"Why not?" asks Sibyl, crossly.

"Oh, because—," replies Molly. "Why because—. Oh, because I never knew people out of a fairy story come to be our next door neighbours. I am a great deal older than you, Sibyl, dear—"

"But you are not as old as Grannie or Uncle Edward," interrupts Sibyl quickly. "And people out of a fairy story might come to be our next door neighbours."

"Yes, they *might*," replies Molly, doubtfully.

"And they must be next door neighbours *somewhere*," argues Sibyl.

"I believe they stay where they are," says Molly, meekly.

"Where is that?" demands Sibyl.

"Why in our book they are next door neighbours to 'Cinderella,' and the 'Yellow Dwarf,'" says Molly, meekly.

"Well, then, they've got tired of living next door to them, and they have come to live next door to *us*," says Sibyl, positively. "The fairies told them we were wery nice, and they've come to see us of their own accord."

"Perhaps they have," says Molly, meekly, but still doubtfully.

"I am sure it was the Beast's legs I saw," says

Sibyl, triumphing over her sister. "Why nobody but a beast would wear *fur* all down to his boots, Molly."

"No, I suppose they wouldn't," says Molly. "Don't you think we could both squeeze into the hole? Perhaps I should see him if I was with you, Sibyl. You *are* lucky."

"Yes, I are," says Sibyl, much pacified. "Let us try, sister."

Jacob has finished his marketing quickly, and is back all too soon. The first thing he does on his return home is to take a walk round his beloved garden to make sure that nothing has happened during his short absence.

Soon he comes upon a hole in the hedge, out of which appear a fat pair of legs, a thin pair of legs, some white petticoats, the upturned soles of two little pairs of shoes, the toes of which are stuck fast in the ground. Jacob's sight is failing, and he thinks they are *cats*.

"If it ain't them nasty white cats of Widow

Wilson's," he mutters to himself, "and they does a sight of mischief, scampering over the flower-beds. Es-ss-sss-ss-sss-sss-sss," and Jacob hisses until he is out of breath.

"They don't take no notice, the impudent things," he mutters. "I must ax the master to let me keep a dog. *He'll* send them to the right-abouts. I'll just fetch a squirt now and give 'em a bit of my mind."

But when Jacob comes back, the cats have turned into two grubby and red-faced little maidens who are shaking the dirt from their dresses, capes, and sun-bonnets. There is a large hole in the hedge, and two of Jacob's finest chrysanthemums are broken off at the roots, and lie upon the ground at his feet.

The old man is extremely cross, but his scoldings fall upon deaf ears. Sibyl is so taken up with Beauty and the Beast, that she hardly hears what he says; while Molly, who only imagines it is his complaint that is troubling him, makes him ten times worse by saying in a pitying voice,

"Poor, poor Jacob."

"A purring over me as if I was one of they nasty cats," grumbles Jacob, as they walk placidly off hand-in-hand. "And never so much as saying they are sorry for the mischief they have done. There! for hard-heartedness, and mischief, and stubbornness, there is nothing equals *girls!* I'd a deal rayther have a dozen boys here for the holidays than they two girls all the year round. Boys *is* wild, but they have their feelings, and that is more than can be said of girls. There's no making no impression on girls, oh no!"

And when next Molly and Sibyl visit their hole for another peep, they find it filled tightly in with the prickliest of brambles Jacob could get—and he went a long way in search of them.

CHAPTER XI.

MOLLY, SIBYL, AND PRINCE CHARMING.

PRINCE Charming is away with his father, upon a visit for a couple of days. Perhaps if he had been at home the little sisters would have been too much occupied with him to think of the mischief into which they are falling, and in that case this story would never have been written.

Grannie has a headache, and is lying down upon her bed. But before she leaves the drawing-room she sees Molly and Sibyl seated upon two hassocks, each with a handkerchief ready to hem. She says she hopes she shall find that Molly has done a whole side, and Sibyl half a side by the time she comes back to her afternoon tea.

MOLLY, SIBYL, AND PRINCE CHARMING.

Grannie has taught each of the sisters to work so soon as they could hold a needle. Sibyl can hem very nicely if she chooses. But to-day she does not choose; she is thinking of Beauty and the Beast. A few minutes pass in silence; then Sibyl looks up from her work and stretches.

"Don't like this work, sister," she says.

"But Grannie wants it done," replies Molly soberly.

"My hands are so sticky," says Sibyl, fretfully.

"So are mine," says Molly.

"And my stuff is hard and stiff."

"So is mine," says Molly.

"*Harder* and stiffer to-day than it ever has been before, sister."

"So is mine," replies Molly.

"I shan't do any more of the nasty thing," and in a temper Sibyl throws the handkerchief upon the floor.

"Oh, Sibyl!" says Molly reproachfully.

"I don't care if I *do* get scolded," says Sibyl petulantly.

"I don't think Grannie ever scolds unless it is for our good," says Molly serenely. "And she is *such* a dear Grannie."

"Yes, she is a wery dear Grannie," says Sibyl in a softer tone, and sucking her thumb.

"And she will be so vexed if we don't do our work, and she said that after we had finished we might amuse ourselves with anything in the room, so long as we're careful," says Molly.

"May we open the drawers of that thing over there?" asks Sibyl.

"Cabinet," suggests Molly.

"Never mind its name. May we?" says Sibyl.

"Yes, if we are careful, and we finish our work *first.*"

"Then I'll work," says Sibyl, dancing joyfully round the room, "and then we'll look in those drawers, sister. Where is my old hankey gone? I wonder."

She picks up her handkerchief, and fetches her workbox, for one of the fairy needles which are usually kept for best. Then she settles down with wrinkled brows and an earnest air.

In twenty minutes the work is finished, the handkerchiefs are folded up, patted down, and put upon Grannie's table.

"Now for the drawers," says Sibyl, leading the way.

The deep drawer is filled with Indian curiosities. Beetles' wings, embroidered bags and slippers, a small case of butterflies, a tiny silver vase chased with gold, a carved ivory paper-knife, &c., &c., &c.

The next drawer is full of Swiss carvings, and lying upon the top is a carved wooden card-case, dark wood with light leaves trailing over it.

"It opens," says Sibyl, pouncing upon it.

"Oh, you have seen that a great many times," says Molly, who is showwoman. "That is only Grannie's card-case." But Sibyl has opened it, and taken out one of the cards. She lays it upon her little hand, which it almost covers.

"Now then, Sibyl, put it back again before I show you anything else," says Molly. "You have looked at it long enough. There is nothing to see in it."

But Sibyl does not stir, she seems fascinated by the card; suddenly she turns upon Molly. A shadow of coming mischief lies darkling in her green eyes.

"Molly," she says, "let us call upon Beauty and the Beast ourselves. We can take one of Grannie's cards and leave it."

"Oh, Sibyl," says Molly, in a shocked voice. "How can you think of such a thing? Put the card-case back at *once*."

"Grannie won't be neighbourly, and we will," persists Sibyl. "Let us go, Molly. I do want so *very* much to see Beauty and the Beast."

If Molly had taken the card-case into her own hands at that moment, had put it into the drawer, and shut the drawer upon it, Sibyl would have pouted and frowned, but would have forgotten the whole affair in a few minutes. But Molly does not do this—she stands still and hesitates.

"It will be lovely," says Sibyl. "We will leave it at the door without going in. Grannie does sometimes, you know, and then they will come and see us, and we shall go and see them."

"Yes, I suppose we should," says Molly slowly. "Because I asked Grannie the other day if she would go and see our next door neighbours if they came to see us, and Grannie said, 'Certainly, my dear.' But suppose dear Grannie should be *vexed*, sister. We should be very sorry if we made her sorry."

"Grannie doesn't know they are Beauty and the Beast," says Sibyl, "and she wouldn't believe if we said they were. But she won't mind when she *does* know, Molly, 'cause she said the other day when I was telling her about Beauty and the Beast—Grannie said—they were wery old friends of hers, and that she knew them when she was quite a little girl. And she likes her old friends, she says she do—"

"Does, not *do*," says Molly. "That's bad grammar."

"Never mind," replies Sibyl.

Now Molly, being older than Sibyl, does not in the least believe it is Beauty and the Beast who have come to be their next door neighbours, but she is quite as anxious as her sister to see *who* it really is: so though a little voice keeps whispering, "Molly, it is wrong; Molly, Molly, you know it is wrong," she will not listen to the little voice, and after a bit it grows slower and fainter, and then dies away altogether.

"If we leave the card, Sibyl," she says, "we will put our names as well as Grannie's. They will like to know we have called as well as Grannie."

"But we can't print," says Sibyl, opening her eyes wide. "The card is print, Molly dear."

"We will write our names under Grannie's name. I have seen Grannie write Cousin Milly's name when she was staying here," says Molly.

"How you 'member things, Molly dear," replies Sibyl admiringly. "Write it in big large writing, not in your beautiful small writing what is so clever that no one can read it."

Molly seats herself in a chair in front of the writing-table, Sibyl kneels down upon a chair by her side. Molly chooses a pen and dips it into the ink.

A large blot falls upon the card.

"That's a kiss," says Sibyl in delight. "The Beast will like to have a kiss. Make another kiss, Molly dear. One from you, and one from me. Oh, and one from Grannie—one, two, three—three. Three kisses—one from each of us."

"That one is so big it will do from all of us," says Molly. "Now don't talk, Sibyl, or I can't write."

Sibyl is quiet as a mouse, and watches with great interest every turn of her sister's pen.

The two names are written under Grannie's—"Molly and Sibyl." Then Molly rests. Both children gaze at it admiringly, and Sibyl gives it a little pat.

"Oh, but you mustn't leave out Prince Charming, Molly," she cries at length. "Put him in now, directly. We mustn't leave him out. He'll like to see the Beast wery, wery much."

"Shall I put 'Arthur,' or 'Prince Charming?'" asks Molly.

"Prince Charming," says Sibyl. "I'll spell it for you, if you don't know how. P-r—"

"Oh, I know," interrupts Molly, and sets to her task again.

"There's another blot," says Sibyl in the highest glee. "That's two big kisses. Now it's quite done. How lovely it looks, Molly dear."

This is the card when Molly has finished it.

> Mrs Edward Barrington.
> Molly and Sybil and
> Prince Charming

"Now double it up," cries Sibyl.

"Oh, but, Sibyl," says Molly very decidedly, "I don't believe Grannie ever doubles up her cards. She gives them in at the door quite *flat*."

"You are not *quite* sure," says Sibyl.

"Very nearly sure," answers Molly, "but not quite certain, positive."

"Grannie doubles up her letters with writing on them," says Sibyl, "and this card has writing upon it. You are not *quite* certain, positive, sister, so we'll double up the card, 'cause it's got writing on it."

"I am *nearly* sure," says Molly, as she unwillingly folds the card in two.

"Now we'll sealing-wax him," says the excited Sibyl, as her glistening eyes catch sight of the sealing-wax.

"You should say 'it' and not 'him,' when you mean *things*,—Uncle Edward says so," replies Molly. "And I am quite sure that Grannie *never* sealing-waxes her cards, *quite* sure."

"It won't stick if it isn't sealing-waxed," cries Sibyl, briskly. "Here are the lucifers. You light one, sister, 'cause when I lighted a lucifer it burnt my finger," and Sibyl nurses her finger and looks grave over the memory of it.

Molly shakes her head and sighs as she takes the lucifer match from her sister's outstretched hand.

"Let me drop the sealing-wax," says Sibyl, quickly. "There, now I've dropped two little drops as well. That's two more kisses. There is a kiss from each of us now, Molly, dear."

The card is ready at last with two kisses in ink, and two in sealing-wax, neatly folded in the middle and sealed with Grannie's crest. This is how it looks when it is doubled up—

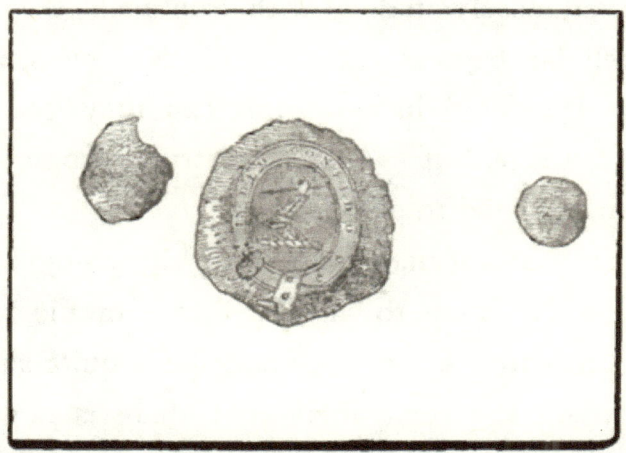

"We can take it after we have had our tea," says Sibyl.

"Let us leave it until to-morrow," suggests Molly. "For I am quite sure Grannie *never* pays visits in the evening, Sibyl."

"Oh, but it must go to-day," says Sibyl, in

feverish haste, "and it need not be evening after tea. We can call it afternoon."

Near upon six o'clock two little figures may be seen stealing in at the iron gates and walking, hand-in-hand, along the short avenue of trees leading to the Red House. But when they reach the big door, closely studded with iron nails, they find the bell far beyond their reach. Not even, when Molly lifts Sibyl in her arms, can they get near enough to pull it. And after trying some time they are obliged to give it up.

"Let us slip it under the door," says Sibyl.

Molly is about to answer that Grannie never slips the cards under the door, she is quite sure of *that*, when she remembers that there is nowhere else where they can put it, for letter-boxes have not reached this part of the world yet. So she says nothing. And the card is slipped underneath the door, with its four names, its four kisses, and its big seal. Who will be the first to find it, Beauty or the Beast? That we shall hear by-and-by.

CHAPTER XII.

THE ROOM WITHOUT A DOOR.

"Oh, Molly Bawn, why leave me pining,
All lonely waiting here for you?"
Old Song.

"PRINCE Charming, I never thought you could be so unkind."

"No, we *never* did."

Outside the gates leading to the Red House is an old tree with thick roots twisting and twining out of one another until they form quite a comfortable seat. It is here that Molly and Sibyl have seated themselves, while, standing beside them, hat in hand, is Prince Charming. The wind blows his yellow curls astray, tears stand in his sweet brown eyes, and his usually pale face is flushed a deep rose-red.

"Oh, Molly," he answers piteously, "I do not want to be unkind. It vexes me so very much that you think me unkind. Dear, dear Molly, I would do *anything* for you."

"No, you will not," answers Molly, "for we have just asked you to pay a visit with us, and you won't come."

"And we wrote your name upon the card and all," says Sibyl's injured voice. "Just pay this one little wisit with us, Prince Charming, and we will never ask you to do nothing again," (in a very coaxing voice.)

"I wish you would ask me to do things," cries Arthur. "You know how much I love you, and how I like to do things for you."

"We don't believe that you love us," says Sibyl obstinately.

"No, we don't," says Molly grimly.

There is a long silence,—such a long silence, and they are all three so quiet, that a mouse ventures out of its hole to peep at them, and then runs away.

"Grannie does not know," says Arthur in a low voice, at last. "Oh, Molly, please give it up."

"We won't give it up," says Molly firmly, "and if you loved us, you would come with us."

"Yes, you would," says Sibyl.

"Father would say it is not right, I am sure he would," replies Arthur as firmly as Molly herself has spoken.

"Come along, Sibyl, it is no use talking to him," and the sisters get up, join hand-in-hand, march past Arthur, push open one of the gates, squeeze through it, and stand upon the other side of them.

Arthur springs forward.

"Stop, Molly, stop!" he cries, beating with his little white hands against the gate which does not open. "Stop just one minute, dear Molly,—I want to say something—I really do."

They are very close to each other as they turn to face him, with only the iron bars of the gate between them. Just for a second they stand gazing into each other's eyes,—Arthur flushed and appealing, stretching out an arm, longing to draw them back; Molly, sturdy and obstinate; Sibyl, wilful and petulant, a pout upon the rose-bud mouth, mischief working in the green eyes.

"You haven't said it," says Molly at length. "What is it?"

"'Cause we are in a hurry," says Sibyl, tossing her head.

"I do not think it is right," says Arthur, in a trembling voice, "and Father told me once that when we do anything that is not right, it takes us a great way off from GOD, and we have to be very, very sorry before we can get quite close to Him again. Dear Molly, you don't want to get a long way off from GOD, I am sure you don't. Do please, *dear* Molly, give it up and come home with me, and we will have such a nice game of play."

Arthur's pleading is so earnest, that for the moment Molly hesitates. A drizzling rain is beginning to fall, and forgetting their quarrel for the moment, she holds out a warning hand.

"Put on your hat at once, Prince Charming, or you will catch cold," she says in her motherly protecting way.

"We have got on our best bonnets," says Sibyl, "won't the rain spoil the feathers, Molly dear?"

"Yes," replies Molly, hastily. "We must hurry," and they turn their backs upon Prince Charming and his pleading face.

"Oh, Molly, don't go," he cries once again. "Come back, Molly. Dear, dear Molly, come back."

"Never," says Molly, as she draws herself up and walks stiffly along the gravel path, "*Never, never, never* will I love my next door neighbour again."

But Arthur does not see, nor Sibyl either, that even as Molly is saying these cruel words, two large tears have gathered in her dark eyes, roll slowly down her cheeks and splash upon her dress.

When they are out of sight Arthur sits down upon the roots of the tree and cries heart-brokenly. He fears he has offended them hopelessly, he knows how much he loves them, and he feels how lonely he shall be without the two sisters to share his interests—much lonelier than ever he was before, because now he will *miss* them, and we cannot miss things we have never had. For full half an hour he sits there in the drizzling rain, shivering, sad, and uncomfortable, keeping a loving, longing, wistful gaze upon the iron gates, hoping every minute that two little white figures will steal through the gloomy trees, and he shall be able to make peace with them.

In the meanwhile Grannie thinks that Molly and Sibyl are safe at Riverside, and Cerisette never dreams but that Arthur is at Shadie Cottage with the sisters—where he is always to be found when he is missing.

Unknown to Maria, the sisters have dressed themselves in their best. They are alike, as usual. Their frocks are white cashmere, trimmed with white silk, and with white capes to match. Their bonnets are drawn white silk with a tiny plume of white feathers upon one side. Their stockings are black silk, and their shoes have black rosettes.

It is not a cheerful afternoon. The wind moans sorrowfully through the branches every now and then, breaking off a dry twig or handful of withered leaves, and dropping it at the children's feet. Overhead dark clouds drift quickly, as if in a hurry to get home. The sky is grey from one end to the other, and the misty rain falls steadily, drearily.

Even fearless Molly shivers as they come in sight of the Red House. It is large and gloomy, the big door in the middle of it closely shut and the windows gazing blankly at them. It has not a neighbourly look. How are they to get in, as they cannot reach to ring the bell?

"There are always two doors to a house,"

says Molly, briskly. "Let us find the other door."

"It will be somewhere round the corner," says Sibyl, and they pass through a trellis-work gate to find themselves in the midst of the garden at the back of the house.

It is a perfect wilderness, but in the orchard beyond the wind is shaking down from the trees whole showers of ungathered fruit. The sisters stand for a few minutes fascinated by the ripe red and golden rain as it patters into the long grass. Then they trot along hand-in-hand to search for the second door.

A square paved-courtyard is before them, which leads them to the back of the house. When they have crossed this they find a stone archway. No one is to be seen, everything is as quiet as the dead of night, and the silence is only broken by the patter of their little feet as they enter under the archway and along a broad stone passage. At the end of this is a flight of stairs with a door at the top; it is not locked, so they push it open and enter. As it shuts behind them it gives such a loud bang that both Molly and Sibyl jump and look at each other in a frightened manner. Just for a minute they hold their breath, then take courage and glance around them. They have two ways from which to choose. To their right are three steps, leading to a long passage with doors on either side. To their left is a long, low flight of stairs leading upwards. Both pairs of eyes seek this staircase, and without speaking they begin to ascend it. It ends in a long corridor, with places for pictures upon one side of it and numbers of doors upon the other.

"There *are* a great many doors," says Sibyl. "Which shall we knock at, Molly dear?"

They knock gently at the first door, then louder, then louder still. But there is no answer, nothing stirs, and all is quiet as the dead of night.

"Perhaps the poor Beast is *ill*, and Beauty can't

leave him," says Sibyl. "Hadn't we better open the door a tiny bit, sister, and look in?"

Molly turns the handle slowly and gently, and the two pairs of curious eyes open wide with astonishment as they look. The room is large and empty, not even a chair to show that it has ever been occupied.

"He is not at home in this room," says Sibyl, "but there is a door in that corner, perhaps he is in that room, sister dear."

They cross the floor which is thickly covered with dust. Sibyl glances at it in disgust, and lifts the skirt of her short white frock daintily up—as if it *could* possibly touch the ground.

"Grannie would scold Ellen if she left all that dust about in our house," she says shaking her head gravely. "I don't think the Beast looks after his servants p'operly, Molly dear."

"Perhaps he does not," answers Molly placidly. Then they knock at the door in the corner of the room, but there is still no answer, and upon opening it, they find it as large, and dusty, and empty as the one they have left behind them.

But there are still doors to tempt them on, and they have crossed eight or ten of these large, empty rooms, most of them with two or three steps leading down into them, when Sibyl comes to a standstill.

"Oh, Molly," she says in a panic of fear, grasping her sister's wrist tightly, "s'pose we shouldn't be able to find our way back again?"

"Oh, yes, it is quite straight," says Molly calmly.

She is not nervous, and it takes a great deal to frighten her. Sibyl's spirits rise as she looks in Molly's face.

"The Beast has plenty of rooms to growl in," she says, jumping daintily over a heap of fluff and dust, "but if we are not clean when we call upon him it will be all his fault for keeping his rooms so dusty. Molly, do you think Grannie would lend him Ellen to clean up for him a bit?"

"Ellen has enough to do to keep our house

clean," says Molly. "No, I don't think Grannie would lend him Ellen, but she might get another Ellen for him, and that would do just as well."

"We will ask her," says Sibyl delightedly. "I 'spect the poor Beast wants amoosing like Prince Charming, and the nice doctor sent him down here for us to be his medicine. Don't you think so, sister dear?"

But Molly does not answer. She is ahead of Sibyl, and she is so accustomed to go out of one large empty room into another that she is surprised when the last door she has opened brings her down three low steps into a narrow oak passage. It is long and dark, but the two sisters grope their way along it until they are stopped by a handle. Molly turns the handle, the door is not locked, but it does not open so readily as the others—something is in the way.

"Perhaps it is a dress," suggests Sibyl, whose eyes and wits are quick. "Cook hangs up her

PAGE 169.

dresses behind the door. The Beast would not wear dresses, but Beauty would. Push hard, sister."

"I think it is a curtain," says Molly, but she pushes hard, and they squeeze through. The door closes behind them with a snap, the curtain falls into its place, and Molly and Sibyl find themselves in a square unfurnished room, the floor of dark oak, and the walls hung from the top to the bottom with tapestry.

"Oh, what lovely pictures!" says Sibyl admiringly. "I wonder if the Beast painted them all himself? I am tired, Molly; I cannot go any further until I am rested. Let us look at the pictures."

"Very well," replies Molly.

The light comes from a window in the roof, there is no fire-place, and each side of the wall is one large picture worked in tapestry.

The first, from which they turn with a shudder, is a battle-field,—a mass of arms and legs, struggling horses, and falling men. Not a pleasant subject to rest your eyes upon.

The second is prettier. Green trees, many coloured flower-beds, and a broad gravel walk leading to a castle with tall towers.

The third is the same castle. A man in bright armour is riding down the gravel path, turning back to wave his hand to a lady, who is leaning over one of the towers throwing kisses to him.

The fourth picture is the same castle again, with the same man in armour, only this time he is riding *towards* the castle, and a great many people are waiting to welcome him. And coming to meet him is the lady who threw kisses to him, carrying a child in her arms, with another clinging to her dress.

"Now we will go," says Sibyl. "How are we to get out? I don't see any door, sister."

"We must lift up the curtains to find the door," says Molly. "How queer it is to paint pictures upon curtains, isn't it, Sibyl?"

"Wery quare indeed," says Sibyl.

"Here is the handle," says Molly cheerfully. "I am glad I have found it, for now we shall not have to go back all through those dusty rooms."

She turns the handle, but the door does not move. She pulls it sharply to try if it is locked,—when it instantly flies open with a whizzing sound; there is a low step, over which they quickly pass, and the door at once closes with the same noise it made when it opened.

They are in a small square-shaped room, lighted from above like the one they have left, and with a dark oak floor. But the walls are covered with pictures,—not pictures hung up, but pictures painted upon the wall. There is not a space an inch square that is left uncoloured. The two sisters for some minutes are lost in admiration, and walk about hand-in-hand looking—and praising.

"I think we had better go on now," says Sibyl rather uneasily.

"Oh, yes," says Molly cheerfully, "for it would

in the welwet coat it is wery rude of him to laugh at us. He ought to help us to find the door. Molly, take me home at once to dear Grannie."

Poor Molly does not answer. She gazes despairingly about her, and then sets to work to press, with her hands all round the room, hoping, against hope, to find the door by which they entered. She does not know that it is cunningly painted into a picture to look as if it were part of the picture. And how they tease her, these pictures, with their merry mocking faces. She is so inclined to cry, but then she must not cry because of Sibyl. If both give way what will become of them? They may stay here for ever and *starve*, for there is no sound or sign of any living creature, though Sibyl's screams must have pierced the thickest walls. She closes her eyes to shut out the sight of the pictures, and then answers cheerfully,

"Don't cry, Sibyl dear, it makes me want to cry too. There must be a door somewhere, and if we got in we are sure to be able to get out."

Then cheered by her own brave words, she goes round and round the room again, hopefully feeling each separate panel.

From underneath her eye-lashes Sibyl watches her, and ceases screaming. But Molly's heart is beating faster, and a frightened look is coming into her roguish blue eyes. Was it true what Prince Charming said? Is it not very wrong of them to disobey Grannie, when Grannie asked them in such a gentle way to trust her and be good little children? Dear Grannie is so kind to them always. And can it be that by being so naughty they have got such a long way off from GOD that He has forgotten them altogether, and will not have them for His little children any more? It is a dreadful thought. Molly draws a long breath, and great tears fill her eyes, but she sends them back with an effort. In the midst of her terror and uneasiness, the brave little woman still keeps up, for Sibyl's sake.

She leans against one of the pictures. Her heart

is beating very fast, but she tries to steady her voice as she says,

"Don't you think, sister, we shall feel better if we say our little hymn that Grannie taught us to say when we are not very well?—

> ' In my little bed I lie,
> Looking up unto the sky.'

That is the one I mean, Sibyl."

"It is wicked to say it," says Sibyl pettishly. "It is telling a story, 'cause I am not lying on my little bed, but on this nasty hard floor, and you are standing on your own two legs, you know you are, Molly."

"Then shall we say Grannie's Psalm—'The LORD is my Shepherd,'" suggests Molly meekly.

"Why should we say it?" asks Sibyl obstinately. "It is not bedtime yet."

Molly is silent, she does not like to frighten Sibyl by telling her the thoughts that have come into her mind, but what is she to do if her sister will not help her by being good and reasonable?

She crosses her hands over her chest, to keep back the sobs that are almost choking her, then shuts her eyes and presses her head against the panel while she begins to say to herself the little hymn. In one minute the picture against which she is leaning gives way with a crack! snap! like the report of a gun, and Molly is jerked backward into another room, falling heavily against a chair. The pain is sharp, but the soft crown of her bonnet saves her from being seriously hurt. Loud, piercing screams warn her that Sibyl is alone in the room without a door; she gets up quickly and finds, to her great relief, that a little piece of her cape has caught in the panel. She pushes it open wider with all her strength, and calls quickly to Sibyl to come, for the door has a spring fastening, and she finds it difficult, though she does not know why, to keep it open. And as she waits for Sibyl, she turns and looks quickly round the room she has so strangely entered.

CHAPTER XIII.

GRANNIE'S VERY OLD FRIEND.

WHAT a comfort it is to see tables, and chairs, and carpets again after passing through so many unfurnished, dusty rooms, and then being shut up in that mysterious room without a door. In spite of her pain, Molly smiles with content as she sees, from the fire which is blazing half way up the chimney and the little round table covered with a white cloth, drawn in front of it, that somebody lives here. The fire looks so comfortable too this chilly autumn evening, with the drizzling rain beating against the window panes, and the wind howling drearily round the house.

Sibyl is very cautious. Before she ventures into another unknown room, she takes a peep first to see what it is like. Just as she does so, a door nearly opposite to them opens, and something large and furry enters, closing the door behind it.

A wild frightened look in Sibyl's eyes makes Molly turn, and she too sees this big, furry figure. In an eager, breathless whisper Sibyl says,

"Oh Molly, it *is* the Beast!"

"Don't be frightened, Sibyl, dear," says Molly, soothingly, though her own heart is beating wildly. "You wanted to see him, you know."

"He's—oh—Molly! Molly!"—(in the same terrified whisper,)—"*He's taking off his skin!*" and Sibyl seizes hold of the first thing she can grasp, which happens to be a lock of Molly's hair. Molly bears the pain without screaming, and only tries to soothe Sibyl.

"But Sibyl, you know, the Beast turned into a handsome Prince," she says.

At this moment the Beast, a tall, big man, with curling hair the colour of a lion's mane, and a heavy moustache to match, catches sight of the two sisters. He is more surprised to see them than they are to see him, and for a few seconds he wonders if he is dreaming or awake.

Sibyl stands in the midst of the open panel, just preparing to step out of it. Her bonnet has fallen to the back of her head, her large curl has come unfastened, and lies in a fluffy, golden-brown wreath across her forehead. Her shadowy eyes are dark with wonder and terror; her lips are parted, as if about to speak. One of her hands grasps Molly's hair, the other supports her against the panel as she bends forward. Molly is turned partly towards Sibyl, her face white with pain, and her large dark eyes gazing protectingly at her. Both the sisters are as still as if they were carved in marble. The Beast shakes himself, then strides across the room to their side.

"Are you *real* children," he says, "and if so, how did you get here?"

At the sound of the friendly voice Sibyl's alarm vanishes.

"What have you done with your skin?" she says, "and why did you take it off?"

"Do you mean my fur coat?" asks the Beast. "I never wear it in the house. It is only for out-of-doors."

"Our book does not say that," says Sibyl, puckering her eyebrows. "But we are wery glad to see you," she continues, with the air of an empress, giving him her tiny hand and stepping quite out of the open panel. Molly is delighted to let it go, for it has been painful work holding it. Now it shuts with the same crack! snap! just as if a pistol were going off.

"Thank you," the Beast replies to Sibyl's remark, and looking amused. Then as his eye falls upon Molly, "But how white you are, my child. Are you ill?"

"I fell down and hurt my head," says Molly, faintly putting up her hand to the back of her head.

The Beast, if it is he, lifts her in his strong arms, sets her in an arm-chair, and gives her a glass of water to drink.

"Now, lie quite still and do not attempt to speak," he says. "Your sister—I suppose she is your sister—will tell me how you came here. Lie quite still and shut your eyes."

Molly does as she is bid, and feels the rest very pleasant, for she was sick and stunned with the pain of her fall. Sibyl seats herself in a low rocking-chair, leans back in it, brings the tips of her fingers together, and looks at the Beast.

"We came to pay you a wisit," she says, "and we couldn't find you. We got into a nasty room without any door, and Molly fell through one of the pictures."

"Ah! The picture-room," says the Beast. "If you once got in *there* I wonder you ever found your way out of it. I should have said it was almost impossible to find the spring unless you knew the secret."

"What secret," inquires Sibyl, curiously.

"I will show you some day, but your sister would like to see too, and she must stay quiet for a while. How did you get into the picture-room?"

"We came through a great many empty rooms, and *very* dusty indeed they were," says Sibyl, in a reproving voice.

"Then you entered by the back of the house," says the Beast, "and how did you get out of the picture-room?"

"It was Molly found the way," replies Sibyl. "She just tumbled through one of the pictures and held it open for me."

"She touched the spring by accident," says the Beast. "You must not think I am not pleased at this unlooked-for visit, if I ask you why you have come to see me. You do not know me, do you?"

"We have never seen you before, Molly and me," says Sibyl, quietly. "But you are a *wery* old friend of Grannie's. She knew you when she was quite a little girl."

"I think she must have made some mistake," says the Beast, "for I was born in Russia and have only just come to England."

"She is not our grannie but our great-grannie," explains Sibyl, "and she is the wery nicest grannie in the whole world."

"Ay," says the Beast, "and how old may your Grannie be? I am afraid it is not a very polite question, but you will excuse it, perhaps."

"Our Grannie was eighty-three her last birthday," says Sibyl, promptly. "But she never gets no older."

"Dear me," says the Beast.

"She always looks the same, never no older, and

she never grows," says Sibyl. "She has always looked the same ever since we came to live with her, and that is a long time, oh, a *very* long time ago."

"I am sure I could not have had the pleasure of knowing your Grannie, perhaps it was my father."

"Oh, but she says so," interrupts Sibyl, indignantly, "and our Grannie *never* tells stories, and she never lets Molly or me tell them. She says it is very wicked. And Grannie said you were a *very* old friend of hers. She knew you when she was quite a little girl. Perhaps you don't 'member, but our Grannie 'members."

"Do you know my name?" asks the Beast.

"Oh, yes," replies Sibyl, readily. "Ever since we looked through the hedge and saw your two furry legs."

"Yes!" says the Beast, "and what is my name?"

"Why, The Beast, of course," says Sibyl, quietly.

At the sound of his own name the Beast starts, then pulls away rather fiercely at his tawny moustache.

"It is the queerest thing I ever heard in my life"—he begins.

"What is quare?" asks Sibyl, in a frightened voice. "You are not cross, are you? 'Cause if you are going to growl, Molly and me would rather go."

"No, no, I am not thinking of growling, I assure you. Sit still and tell me why you call me by that—unpleasant name?"

"Why it is your name," says Sibyl. "You are the Beast. You have changed into a handsome Prince now, only you will be the Beast again when you put on your skin. But where is *Beauty?* Hasn't her papa stolen the roses yet?"

At this the Beast laughs—a hearty, ringing laugh; and Sibyl, much offended, sucks her thumb, and looks gravely at him.

"*Now* I see it all. It is as clear as daylight," he says. "I am sorry to disappoint you, but I must tell you the truth. I am not the Beast, nor any relation of that worthy animal. What you thought was my skin is only a fur coat I bought in Russia, and which I am fond of wearing if it is in the least cold, for I am a very chilly person. My real, true name is Valentine Gordon."

Things real and unreal are most strangely mixed in Sibyl's little head this evening. She gives one startled glance at him, and takes her thumb quickly out of her mouth.

"A walentine!" she exclaims. "One of those things they sealing-wax and send by post? Oh, I *wouldn't* be sealing-waxed and sent by post, if I were you. It must hurt you wery much, I am sure," in a tone of great alarm.

"No, no," says Mr. Gordon soothingly. "I am never sent by post. My Christian name is Valentine, just as your sister's is Molly, and yours is ———, by the way, you have not told me your name yet?"

"You know my name," says Sibyl. "It was on the card we left."

"What card?" he asks. "I saw no card."

"When we called upon you," says Sibyl. "There was Grannie and me and Molly, and Prince Charming."

"Ah, I remember now. It was put under the door and doubled up. 'Molly and Sibyl, and Prince Charming.' You are Sibyl, here is Molly, but where is Prince Charming?"

"We couldn't get him to come," says Sibyl, shaking her head gravely. "But did you see the kisses we sent you?"

"Kisses, no!" he answers.

"One from me, one from Grannie, one from Molly, and one from Prince Charming. Two blots of ink, and two sealing-wax blots."

"Ah! I am very ignorant, and I was not aware those were meant for kisses," says Valentine Gordon meekly. "I am sorry I did not return your visit, but it is not usual to notice cards that are pushed *under* the door."

"We couldn't reach the bell, and we do know how to behave p'operly, 'cause we go to pay wisits with Grannie," Sibyl explains wistfully.

"The bell *is* high," he says; "we must have it altered in some way."

"We put on our best dresses to wisit you to-day," says Sibyl. "Grannie only lets us wear them for *wery* best, 'cause she says its 'travagant. And your rooms were *wery* dusty."

"I hope you did not soil your pretty white frocks, the prettiest I have seen for a long time," he says.

"We held them up," says Sibyl gravely.

"They do not sweep the ground at any rate," he says, trying to hide a smile.

"They come just down to our knees," says Sibyl. "Grannie likes to see our legs, she says. Would you like Grannie to lend you Ellen to clean the rooms? She is a wery good housemaid, Grannie says so."

"Thank you," he says smiling. "But we have engaged our servants, and I hope the rooms will be furnished and clean by the time you come to see me again. I have been up in London choosing furniture, and I have only just run down here now and then. I am the eldest of a large family. They are all abroad at present, but when the house is ready they will come to fill it, and you will be surprised to find what a number of us there are."

"Then you don't live by yourself?" asks Sibyl.

"Oh, no. What should I do with such a huge house? There are sixteen of us altogether," he replies.

"My head is almost well," says Molly, whose colour has come back, "and we must go, because Grannie does not know where we are. We are naughty," she says, turning grave, sorrowful eyes, with not a sparkle of roguishness in them upon Valentine Gordon. "We are *very* naughty. We did not obey dear Grannie, and we shall have made her so sorry."

Sibyl hangs her head, when she sees Valentine Gordon's astonished look.

"Then I am sure you ought to go at once," he says. "I hope your Grannie has not been anxious yet. Do you live far?"

"Only next door," says Molly.

"Shall I take you?" he asks.

"Oh, no, thank you, we would rather go by ourselves. We will run very fast," says Molly.

He shakes hands gravely with both of them. They are very much ashamed of themselves as they run silently home.

At the door they stop.

"He never said he hoped he should see us again," says Sibyl in a tearful voice.

"We have been very naughty," says Molly, "and now we've got to tell Grannie."

"That is the bad part of it," says Sibyl. "Can't we wait a weeny bit, sister dear?"

"Oh, no," replies Molly. "We had better do it at once."

CHAPTER XIV.

GETTING BACK.

AS they enter the house they are met by Maria. "Who ever put you on your best dresses to go and play with Master Arthur?" she exclaims, lifting her hands. "There! your grandmamma *will* be put about."

"But our best dresses is not the worst,—there is a great deal worse to come," says Sibyl gloomily.

"What is the matter?" begins Maria, but the sisters slip past her into the drawing-room.

And whom do you think they see there quietly reading the newspaper to Grannie? Whom but Uncle Edward? He came this afternoon without sending a letter first to say he was coming. He wanted to take them by surprise.

Sibyl plucks Molly's dress.

"Let us wait to tell Grannie until *after* Uncle Edward has gone away again."

But Molly shakes her head, sorrowfully, yet decidedly.

"You never thought you should see *me* to-day," says Uncle Edward, opening wide his arms.

He is prepared for a shout of welcome, a glad rush, and then to be smothered in kisses. He is much surprised to see the sisters stand hand-in-hand in the middle of the room, and make no attempt to draw nearer. Molly is very pale, and her blue eyes are cloudy.

"What ever ails the children?" cries Uncle Edward, while Grannie sits upright in her chair, and says in a quavering voice,

"Oh, my loves, I hope you have not hurt yourselves?"

"We are two wery bad little girls," says Sibyl,

flinging herself recklessly into the midst of the story before Molly can speak. "We dressed ourselves in our best dresses when Maria was not looking, and we didn't trust Grannie, and we went to call upon the Beast—no, the Walentine I mean, he turned into a Walentine, only we thought he was the Beast when we went to wisit him. And we got into a room without any door, and Molly tumbled through the picture and knocked her head. That's all, Grannie."

"Oh, my dears," says Grannie, much distressed, "I cannot make out what you have been about. Nothing wrong, I hope? Why, they have," says Grannie, putting on her spectacles to look at the children closely, "—yes, Edward, they really have on their best frocks and bonnets! Where have you been, my dears?"

"Molly, you are the eldest,—explain to us quietly what you have been about," says Uncle Edward.

"I can 'splain things as well as Molly," murmurs Sibyl indignantly.

"We wanted Grannie to call upon our next door neighbour," says Molly's ashamed voice, speaking fast and low, "and Grannie wouldn't call, and she said we must trust her. And we didn't trust dear Grannie, and we were very naughty one day, and we left Grannie's card at the Red House, and wrote our names upon it too."

"Left my card at the Red House!" murmurs Grannie; "why I never heard of such a thing!"

"Nor I," says Uncle Edward gravely. "Go on, Molly."

"And to-day we went to call, and we couldn't reach the bell, and we went round to the back door. Then we went through a great many rooms with no furniture, and then we got into a picture room, and we couldn't get out,—and then I fell through one of the pictures into another room, and a gentleman came, and he was very kind. We told him we had been very naughty, and that you didn't know we had come, dear Grannie."

Before the last words are finished tears are raining down Molly's cheeks and splashing upon her pretty white dress. Sibyl clings to her, half-frightened herself, but more frightened at seeing brave Molly in tears.

"Now do not cry, my dear," said Grannie, "or you will make yourself ill. It was naughty of you both to disobey me, and to call upon people when I told you there were very good reasons why I did not wish to call. But if you are sorry for what you have done, and will promise to try to be better children for the future, I will forgive you. Say you are sorry, and come and kiss me."

They run joyfully to Grannie, and kiss her upon each of her cheeks, Molly still sobbing bitterly as she thinks how kind Grannie is and what bad children they are ever to have dreamt of disobeying her.

"Now sit down, and let us talk a bit," says Grannie. "I cannot understand, my dears, what made you so anxious to call upon the people at the Red House?"

"I can tell you, Grannie," says Uncle Edward. "It was curiosity was at the bottom of the whole affair. I have told you often that there can be no two people in the whole wide world, so curious as Molly and Sibyl."

"It was 'cause we wanted to be neighbourly," says Sibyl, shaking her head gravely. "Grannie has always said we were to love our neighbours, Uncle Edward."

"Yes, my dear," says Grannie, "and I hope you always will love your neighbours, but I do not call it loving your neighbours to pry into things they may not want you to know."

"What is it to *pry?*" asks Sibyl.

"It means *peeping*," says Uncle Edward. "Such as making a hole in the hedge to see what your neighbours are about."

Molly and Sibyl look into each other's eyes, and then hang down their heads.

"There once lived a *very* good man," says Uncle Edward, "and this good man had a very great friend—at least one who *called* himself a very great friend. And this friend wanted to find out if this good man was just as good when he was quite alone, as he was when many people were watching him. His bedroom was next door to that of this good man, and this very great friend bored a hole in the wall, that he might *peep* through it, and see what the good man did when he was alone. He peeped, and peeped, and he saw that he was the same when he was alone as when he was with a crowd of people. Then he was satisfied, and left off prying. But I always have thought that a man who could do a thing of that sort was not a true friend—not neighbourly, as Sibyl put it— because he did 'not do unto his friend as he would have wished his friend to do unto him.' That is the golden rule, and a very safe rule it is. For I am quite sure this so-called friend was the last person who would have liked to have been watched himself."

"Molly and me wouldn't mind anybody making a hole and watching *us*," says Sibyl.

"Perhaps not," says Uncle Edward. "But when you grow older you will learn that sometimes the truest way to show our love to our neighbour is by leaving him alone. Grannie was anxious you should trust her. She has lived long in the world, and she knows its ways, and she quite understands that sometimes people come to a strange part of the country to be by themselves for a time, and she thought this might be the case with the people who have taken the Red House. But this afternoon a letter came from a lady Grannie knew years ago, saying that the people who have taken the Red House are great friends of hers, and asking Grannie to call. See, my children, how you would have been rewarded if you had trusted Grannie and been patient."

The sisters hang their heads, and say nothing.

"They are a large family," says Uncle Edward, "but at present the eldest son is attending to the furnishing, and they are not ready for visitors."

"Ah, the Walentine," murmurs Sibyl sleepily. "He said he was going to clean up the rooms, they were *wery* dusty, and I said you would lend him Ellen, Grannie."

"My dear, *what* have you been promising? I could not spare Ellen on *any* account," says Grannie distressed.

"No, no, dear Grannie," says Molly soothingly. "He said he didn't want Ellen. He has some servants coming."

A knock at the door.

"The young ladies' tea is quite ready," says Maria.

"Run up at once, my dears," says Grannie, "I am sure you must want your tea. Is your head bad now, Molly?"

"Only a little, thank you, Grannie," says Molly. "Have you forgiven us, Uncle Edward?" she asks, timidly.

"Oh, yes," he says, gathering them both into his arms. "But you must remember that to be *curious* is not to be neighbourly, and that the best part of loving your neighbour is that it teaches you to do kind things at the *right* time—not at the wrong time—and to the right people. And until you grow quite old and able to judge for yourselves, you must trust Grannie and me. *Trust* without asking for reasons, without saying 'Why mustn't I?' or 'Why won't you?'"

"Yes, Uncle Edward," says Sibyl.

"We won't forget," whispers Molly, and the two pairs of arms twine round his neck, and the two white bonnets rest upon his shoulders for a minute in satisfied content.

The sisters are in bed and Sibyl is already nearly asleep, when suddenly she opens one eye and murmurs lazily,

"Sister, are you awake?"

"Yes," replies Molly. "*Very* wide-awake."

"I'm asleep," says Sibyl. "*Wery* nearly. But

Molly dear, I am so sorry I was so c'oss to you in the picture room to-day."

"Never mind," says Molly. "I have forgotten all about it."

"If you are wide enough awake, could you get out of bed and kiss me to make it up?" murmurs Sibyl.

Molly is upon her feet in a second, and running to her sister's bed she presses a kiss upon her soft cheek. Sibyl is so sleepy that she can only throw one arm lazily around Molly's neck ; then it falls upon the counterpane, and she is fast asleep.

Not so Molly. Even after she goes back to bed, she cannot sleep. She lies tossing restlessly from side to side, seeming always to hear Arthur's words —" Molly, Molly, come back, you are going such a long way off from GOD."

She went a long way off from GOD. Has she got near to Him again?

After some time she jumps up, opens the door softly, then runs down stairs into the dining-room where Grannie is eating her supper while Uncle Edward has his dinner.

"Oh, my dear," says Grannie, "what brings you down here in your night-dress, and with your bare feet? what a cold you will catch:" while Uncle Edward seizes a knitted coverlet from the sofa and wraps it around her.

"Grannie," says Molly, nestling timidly to her, "Arthur said to-day that when we do naughty things it takes us a great way off from GOD. And I want to know how to get near to Him again?"

"Did Arthur go with you to the Red House? You never told me *that*, my love," says Grannie.

"No, he wouldn't go. We tried hard to make him, and I was very cross with him because he wouldn't go," says Molly, with tears in her eyes and quivering lips. "He was a good little boy, and he said that you and his papa would not like it, and that it was wrong, and that doing naughty things took us such a long way off from GOD.

And we were in the picture room and couldn't get out, and I thought we had gone such a long way off from GOD that He had forgotten us altogether."

"That would be sad indeed. The saddest thing that could happen, my love," says Grannie, tenderly. "But He had not forgotten you, for He showed you the way out of the room, did not He?"

"Yes, Grannie," replies Molly. "And now I want to get near to Him again."

"And on Sunday," says Grannie, "you read about a child who went a long way off from his father. What did that child say when he was near enough to speak to his father again?"

"I know, Grannie," says Molly. "It was the Prodigal Son; and he said, 'Father, I have sinned.'"

"And what did you say to me this evening after you had told me what you had done?" asks Grannie.

"Dear Grannie, we are so *very* sorry," murmurs Molly, softly.

"Go to your room, my dear," says Grannie, "and kneel down and tell GOD how naughty you have been—just as you told me, and say to Him just what you said to me, and ask Him to help you to be a better child for the future. Then you will have got near to Him again, never, I hope, to go far away from Him any more. And in a few minutes," continues Grannie, "I will come and tuck you up in bed and give you a good-night kiss."

"Thank you, dear Grannie," says Molly, brightly, and with an embrace, as she passes him, to Uncle Edward, Molly runs quickly away.

CHAPTER XV.

JACOB'S LITTLE GIRLS.

IT is two days after Molly and Sibyl paid that never-to-be-forgotten visit. Grannie has settled herself for a comfortable afternoon. She is leaning back in her arm-chair cutting up flannel into the smallest of pieces, to stuff cushions for poor people. It makes such soft cushions, and Grannie is glad to rest her eyes from knitting and other work. Uncle Edward is in a chair by her side, he has a paper-knife in his hand with which he is preparing to cut the leaves of a new book he is just about to read to Grannie.

The door gently opens, and a small figure with a grave face sidles in sideways. This is Molly. Close behind her is another small figure with an equally grave face. This is Sibyl. Hand-in-hand they solemnly cross the room, and stand before Grannie.

"*Is* anything the matter?" asks Uncle Edward, speaking in an I-have-made-up-my-mind-for-the-worst tone of voice.

"Nothing is the matter," says Sibyl, lifting one shoulder much higher than the other; "but we are 'fraid,—at least Molly is 'fraid, *I* isn't."

"Afraid of what?" says Uncle Edward.

"We want to go into the village," says Molly, "and we are afraid—"

"You *was*, I wasn't," says Sibyl boldly.

"*What* grammar!" says Uncle Edward with a shudder. "It is a good thing you are going to have some regular lessons. Now, Molly."

"We thought," says Molly, "that perhaps Grannie would think it *curious*, or naughty to want to know if Mrs. Grey's cold is better,—and Billy Bobbins who broke his arm—"

"And Widow Wilson's little black pig with the curly tail," says Sibyl eagerly. "When we went there last, Widow Wilson said he was off his feed, and wouldn't touch a bite of nothing, and she was 'fraid he was wery ill indeed."

"My dears," says Grannie, "it is never curious or wrong to do kind things, or say kind things to people—"

"At the right time," says Uncle Edward.

"Yes, at the right time," says Grannie. "And I am sure this is the right time, if Mrs. Grey's cold is bad, to send her a pot of currant jelly, for her colds are always in the throat. And Billy Bobbins is a good little boy in the choir, he shall have the custard pudding we did not eat at luncheon to-day, and a pot of raspberry jam, and some plum cake,—he will enjoy those. Ask cook to pack them nicely in a basket for you, and to cut a very large slice of cake."

"A *very* large slice," says Sibyl with glistening eyes. "May he have *half* the cake, Grannie?"

"Well, my dear, a quarter will be enough, I think; and you can take him some more when cook makes a new cake," says Grannie.

"As the little black pig with the curly tail has such a delicate appetite at present," says Uncle Edward, "perhaps he would like a custard pudding. What do you say, Sibyl?"

"I think he would wery much," says Sibyl. "May we ask cook to make him one, Grannie?"

"Oh, Sibyl," says Molly, "don't you know that when Uncle Edward looks so grave, he is only telling make-believes, and not real things?"

"The custard pudding would be wasted on the little pig, my dear," says Grannie, settling herself comfortably in her chair. "I dare say you will find him quite well to-day. Now run off, my loves, and be home in good time for tea."

"Oh, yes, because Prince Charming is coming," says Molly.

"One minute," says Uncle Edward, as they fervently kiss him, "as you are rather more subdued to-day, and not quite such a couple of scaramouches, I want to tell you something. There is a neighbour of yours, a *next* door neighbour too, to whom you are *not* neighbourly."

"Do you mean the walentine?" says Sibyl, "'cause Grannie—"

"I do not mean the 'walentine,' but a much nearer neighbour than the 'walentine,'—I mean Jacob," says Uncle Edward.

"Oh, but he is so c'oss. It's his complaint what is so c'oss," says Sibyl.

"I am afraid you are a great trouble to him, poor old man," says Uncle Edward. "It is not loving your neighbour to treat him as you have treated Jacob. You have not been kind to him, my little girls, you have not done to him as you would have him do to you."

"He hasn't been kind to us," says Sibyl, eagerly. "I am sure if he had wanted the big squirt or the short ladder I would have lent them to him in a minute. He is *never* neighbourly to us, Uncle Edward."

"What have we done to him, Uncle?" asks Molly, wistfully.

"I cannot tell you *everything*," says Uncle Edward, caressing her soft hair. "But I will name a few things. Scampering over the beds when Jacob has dug them up and raked them over—"

"That was when we were playing hide-and-seek," says Sibyl.

"Picking some of his choicest flowers, pulling others up by the roots—"

"That was when we think they is weeds," says Sibyl.

"Running off with his tools, playing ball on forbidden ground, and breaking some of the panes of glass in the forcing frames—"

"That was only once, or twice, or three times when we fur-got," says Sibyl.

"What shall we do, Uncle Edward?" asks Molly.

"Say you are sorry for what you have done, and that you will be better children for the future. Make him happy by promising him not to pick the flowers that he says you may not; and ask him whether a thing *is* a weed before you pull it up, and keep away from the glass frames when you are playing ball."

"It is a wery hard and wery long promise, and perhaps we shall fur-get," says Sibyl.

"You must try and remember," says Uncle Edward. Then they kiss him and trot away.

They pay their visit to Jacob upon their road home. The old man is sitting in his deep, wicker chair, enjoying a pipe before he has his tea. The sisters have seldom been in his cottage before, and they glance around them curiously. It is small, but clean and tidy, and a bright fire burns in the tiny grate.

"We are come to say we are wery sorry," begins Sibyl, briskly.

The old man lifts himself out of his chair.

"And what have you been up to *now*," he says, in an agitated voice. "Is it the—"

"No, no, Jacob, sit down again," says Molly. "We have not done anything at all to-day, but Uncle Edward sent us to tell you we have not been neighbourly and kind to you, and we are going to be better children, and not pick the flowers when you say we mustn't, and not pull up the weeds without asking you if they are flowers—"

"And not run over the beds when you have made them tidy," puts in Sibyl.

"And not play at ball among the frames," finishes Molly.

Jacob's face brightens—then clouds over.

"You'll be forgetting all about it after a day or two, I'll be bound," he says.

"No, no, Jacob, we will try hard to remember," says Molly, earnestly.

"Then I'll be the man to trust you, Miss Molly,"

says Jacob, "and if you keep your promise, I'll end my days in peace, and have never so much as a care upon me."

"'Cept your complaint," says Sibyl.

"Oh, I am so used to him that I don't lay no account by him," says Jacob. "'Twas those teeny hands of yours what were the plague of my life, my little ladies. Many a night I've lain awake worriting over the mischief they teeny hands of yours have done."

"Were we as bad as that?" asks Molly wistfully.

"You see," says old Jacob, "I've neither wife nor children, and this garden it's just wife and child to me. I watch the flowers coming open just as people watch their children growing up, and then just as the flowers is opening to purfection two pairs of little hands pull off the beautiful blossoms, and there! they are gone in the twinkling of an eyelid. If you had only cut 'em off with a knife, I think I could have borne it better, but to pull 'em off as if they was nasty weeds! Why it went to my heart it did, and it went very nigh to breaking of it sometimes it did," and the old man draws the sleeve of his coat across his eyes.

"Oh, Jacob, *don't* cry," says Sibyl hastily. "Where's my hankey gone? Oh, I 'member now, I needled it on to one of my doll's dresses for a train. Have you got your hankey, sister?"

"I don't want a pocket-hankey, thank you, Miss Sibyl," says Jacob, taking up his pipe again. "Now you've given me your promise I'll be a happier man. Why my flowers will be the pride of the county if only you'll let 'em 'bide. I took the first prize for chaney-asters, and them two chrysanthemums what you broke off at the roots when you made that hole in the hedge were finer than any what were at the show."

"Poor Jacob," says Molly penitently. "We did not know you minded so much. We are very sorry, and we *will* be careful, we really will."

"I'll trust you, Miss Molly," says Jacob in a satisfied voice.

"I tell you what, Jacob," says Sibyl eagerly, "we will be really and truly neighbourly. You are all by yourself, and you have no little children. We will come and live with you, and be your two little girls. Won't that be nice for you, Jacob?"

But the old man grows pale.

"You are not in earnest, Miss Sibyl."

"Really and truly," answers Sibyl?

"I wouldn't have you for a mint of money," says Jacob, shaking his grey head vigorously. "Why I should be in my grave in a week. Bless you, Miss Sibyl, *what should* I do with you?"

"Wouldn't you like to have us?" asks Sibyl, in *such* a disappointed voice.

"No, no, my little ladies," says the old man. "You stay where GOD has put you. Why I shouldn't know a minute's rest or peace if you were my little children. I wouldn't have the care of you for a week if I was paid for it in as much gold as I could carry on my shoulders in a sack."

This is plain speaking. Sibyl looks very crestfallen. Molly is thinking sad thoughts, for her eyes are grave.

They both cough.

"There! I ought to have put out my pipe," says the old man apologising. "But I ain't used to ladies visiting me in my house, that's the truth of it."

"We don't mind the baccy—much. But it doesn't smell nice like Uncle Edward's seg-gars," says Sibyl.

"I'll put it away next time you come to see me," says Jacob.

"May we come again?" asks Molly meekly.

"Oh, yes, if you please, little ladies," says old Jacob; "and if your grandma will let you perhaps you will have a cup of tea with me. I've had some rare fine honey sent me from my sister in Scotland, where the bees is fed from the heather—"

"Grannie is sure to let us," says Sibyl briskly, "oh may we come to-morrow, Jacob, and bring Prince Charming with us?"

"Oh, yes," says Jacob, "and the little gentleman is right welcome, for a nicer behaved little gentleman couldn't be found."

"Would you like him for your little boy, Jacob?" asks Sibyl wistfully.

Jacob does not answer.

"We must go," says Molly, "or Prince Charming will be waiting."

"Oh, Jacob," says Sibyl, running back and putting her head in at the door, "you must be neighbourly as well as us, and lend us the big squirt and short ladder when we want them."

"You won't take them without asking, Miss Sibyl?"

"N . . . o," answers Sibyl.

"Then we will see what you want them for afore I lend them to you," says old Jacob.

The sisters are unusually silent that evening, especially Molly. After tea Prince Charming is sitting upon the large old-fashioned sofa, a sister upon each side of him.

"Prince Charming," says Sibyl suddenly, patting his hand as it lies in hers, "you love us wery much, don't you?"

"Very, very much," he answers earnestly.

"Next best to your papa?"

"Oh, yes," says Prince Charming.

"And we have done you a great deal of good?" asks Sibyl again.

"A great deal of good,—everybody says so," replies Prince Charming.

"And we are *wery* nice medicine. Wery nice indeed, are we not, dear Arthur?"

"Very, very nice," Prince Charming tries to answer. But Sibyl has wound her arms tightly round his neck, and Molly is arranging his back curls with her little motherly hand, so he can only make a sound which is more like a grunt than anything else.

But Sibyl—who draws his face close down to hers, and Molly—who pulls back his yellow curls to press a fervent kiss upon his forehead, are both equally satisfied.

Ah! the eerieness is creeping away just as slowly as it came on, and I am waking up to my own world, and leaving the world into which the fairies have taken me far, far away.

Not another word will the fairies tell me to-day. The sweet, silver chiming of their voices has ceased, and I just feel their gauzy wings sweep across my cheek as they flutter past me. Perhaps if I do not move, and open my eyes a little bit, I shall catch a glimpse of them—perhaps see the shining of their diamond crowns, a fragment of their silver trains, a brown curl, or a golden curl whisking out of sight.

Ah! no. The fairies have vanished with the story, and there is nothing of them to be seen. I do not know what you think, but it seems to me they have left it in a very unfinished state. I always imagined that the fairies' stories ended so charmingly, that everybody lived happily ever after.

But may be, as this story is about real people, the fairies prefer to leave it without an end. For they know that none of our stories—the stories of real men, women, and children—ever finish in this world. Now GOD goes into His garden and picks first a rose, then a lily, but our stories will not end until He has folded all His dear ones in His Arms—until He has sent north and south, east and west, to gather His flowers into one splendid nosegay, which will shine and glisten with a thousand starry colours in His beautiful home. And then, but not until then, will it be true of us that "we lived happily ever after."

And *if,*—it is a tiny word, but a very hopeful

one sometimes,—if the fairies at some future time should whisper to me any more of the story, I will not forget, you may be sure, to tell it to you again. For I know you will like to hear, just as I shall, everything that the fairies can find out to tell us about

Molly, Sibyl, and Prince Charming.

www.ingramcontent.com/pod-product-compliance
Lightning Source LLC
Chambersburg PA
CBHW021813230426
43669CB00008B/733